GALVESTON AND THE 1900 STORM

~

GALVESTON AND THE 1900 STORM

Catastrophe and Catalyst

PATRICIA BELLIS BIXEL AND
ELIZABETH HAYES TURNER

June 27, 2000
For Rusti and Susan
Best wishes
Patricia Bellis Bixel
Elizabeth Hayes Turner

University of Texas Press, Austin

This book has been published with the assistance of a grant from the Galveston Historical Foundation.

First edition, 2000

Requests for permission to reproduce material from this work should be sent to Permissions, University of Texas Press, Box 7819, Austin, TX 78713-7819.

∞ The paper used in this book meets the minimum requirements of ANSI/NISO z39.48-1992 (R1997) (Permanence of Paper).

DESIGN AND TYPOGRAPHY BY TERESA W. WINGFIELD

LIBRARY OF CONGRESS CATALOGING-IN-PUBLICATION DATA

Bixel, Patricia Bellis, 1956–
    Galveston and the 1900 storm : catastrophe and catalyst / Patricia Bellis Bixel and Elizabeth Hayes Turner.—1st ed.
        p.   cm.
    Includes bibliographical references (p.   ) and index.
    ISBN 0-292-70883-1 (cl. : alk. paper)
    ISBN 0-292-70884-X (pbk. : alk. paper)
    1. Galveston (Tex.)—History—20th century. 2. Hurricanes—Texas—Galveston—History—20th century. 3. Floods—Texas—Galveston—History—20th century. I. Turner, Elizabeth Hayes. II. Title.

F394.G2 B59 2000
976.4'139—dc21   99-087876

For the victims—and survivors—of the 1900 Storm

SEPTEMBER 8, 1900–SEPTEMBER 8, 2000

∼

CONTENTS

FOREWORD

This is the story of the death and resurrection of an American city. The advent of the twenty-first century marks the centennial of the nation's worst recorded natural disaster, a devastating hurricane that has come to be known as the 1900 Storm. This occasion is an especially appropriate time for a detailed examination and interpretation of how the hurricane that destroyed Galveston, Texas, on September 8, 1900, brought about a political, gender, racial, and technological transformation. An island city located along the southeast coast of Texas, Galveston in 1900 had a population of almost thirty-eight thousand people. It was a cosmopolitan and economically vibrant locale, thanks in good part to its prominence as the state's leading seaport. Yet the geographic features that helped sustain its economic lifeblood also provided the seeds of its destruction. Galveston stood approximately nine feet above sea level on a sandbar island that was prone to flooding. In September 1900 an intensifying tropical disturbance passed from the Caribbean into the Gulf of Mexico and sealed its doom.

Through many firsthand accounts, Patricia Bellis Bixel and Elizabeth Hayes Turner paint a terrifying picture of the hurricane's wrath. Survivors found safe haven in tall buildings as wind and water left the city in ruins. Approximately six thousand people died; thousands more were injured. Estimates of property losses ran as high as $30 million. Wreckage filled the city's streets; corpses and animal carcasses blanketed Galveston with a terrible stench and posed the serious threat of disease. In less than a day, the cataclysm had completely rent the community's fabric. Following the storm,

Galveston was put under martial law to restore order and counter looting. A Central Relief Committee consisting of Mayor Walter C. Jones and eight other civic leaders served to expedite the recovery. Readers of *Galveston and the 1900 Storm* will easily visualize the enormous burden resting on the shoulders of these men as they coordinated efforts to dispose of bodies, rebuild structures, and restore services. Their determination to restore their city was, fortunately, unfettered by partisan bickering.

The disaster brought Clara Barton, then head of the American National Red Cross, to Galveston. Highly respected nationally for her humanitarian efforts, she was a personal catalyst for recovery. Working within the confines of the prevailing male leadership of the city, Clara Barton and the Red Cross assumed responsibility for relief distribution. Although women would be denied the right to vote until 1920, Barton's presence inspired Galveston women to become substantially involved in the shaping of public policy. They assumed a leadership role by evaluating both the losses of their community and the needs of storm survivors. They organized the Women's Health Protective Association in 1901, which had a political agenda from its inception and involved itself in lobbying for adoption of sanitary regulations. Its focus was natural in light of Progressivism's emphasis on "municipal housekeeping." Thereafter, it undertook other causes, such as reburying storm victims and promoting the commission form of local government. In 1912, women assumed a more militant stance toward the issue of suffrage and organized the Galveston Equal Suffrage Association.

Galveston's African American citizens did not fare as well as white women. In 1898, two years before the storm, Galveston blacks lost their most prominent leader with the death of Norris Wright Cuney, who had commanded the respect of the city's influential white powerbrokers. Immediately after the storm, Galveston's black citizens—many of whom had performed heroic rescues—were vilified in the local press as scavengers and looters or portrayed as lazy and childlike. Discriminatory practices in the distribution of relief supplies and donations also worked against African Americans, who received only what was left over—if that.

And, after 1900, blacks had little say in Galveston politics because the commission form of local government, adopted in 1901, required commissioners to be elected at large, thereby effectively depriving blacks of representation. African Americans refused to be passive victims, however, and protested their exclusion both through active lobbying before the commission and through newspaper editorials. In addition, thriving black businesses, churches, and schools gave black Galvestonians a means of achieving self-sufficiency and expressing their pride.

The commission form of government was generally effective—even if, as noted, it excluded Galveston's black population from political representation. The commission was a governing body composed of five men and represented a radical effort to reinvent local government. Before the storm, the city was governed through a traditional mayor and city council structure which in Galveston's case was characterized by gross inefficiency and political infighting. The commission, which included prominent Galveston businessmen, put the city on a firmer, more businesslike footing and enabled the city to cope better with the staggering debt incurred as a result of the storm and the ensuing recovery efforts.

Protecting the city from future hurricanes required particularly drastic solutions, including the construction of a sea wall and the elevation of the city's grade—truly monumental undertakings. Constructed of concrete, the first sea wall segment was three miles long. After this first stage was completed in 1904, subsequent extensions of the wall ultimately ran its length to ten miles, with the final section completed in 1962. The grade raising, the initial portion of which was completed in 1911, entailed moving 16.3 million cubic yards of dredged fill and raising structures, streets, streetcar tracks, water mains, and gas lines. During the period it was under way, this civil engineering feat radically transformed the city's appearance: Galveston truly became "a city on stilts," as it was called. Even by today's standards, the process of elevating over two thousand structures is a mind-boggling accomplishment.

Much scholarly work has been done on the Storm of 1900; *Galveston and the 1900 Storm* makes an important contribution to this area of research, for, unlike earlier works, it is a long-term study of the hurricane, its aftermath, and Galveston's subsequent transformation. From 1900 to 1915, the city was a nexus for certain Progressive Era activities—public health reforms, "municipal housekeeping," and woman suffrage—then sweeping the country. In the process of becoming a progressive southern city, Galveston served, as Bixel and Turner put it, as "a laboratory of sorts, a testing ground for new ideas about government, society, and technology." The authors have made full use of available documentary sources. They mined the holdings of the Rosenberg Library's Galveston and Texas History Center, which has the most significant archives of the 1900 Storm, as well as other research collections nationwide.

Readers will find *Galveston and the 1900 Storm* valuable in many respects. It is a fine history of one of the most historically important and interesting Texas cities. It gives historical information on women and women's groups, African Americans, and politics. (The authors have done an especially admirable job in reconstructing the attitudes held by Galveston's blacks from meager available sources.) And it tells the story of a major natural disaster and recovery.

Perhaps most important, though, *Galveston and the 1900 Storm* is a profile in leadership. Faced with an enormous tragedy, men and women worked in unison to put Galveston back on its feet. They made critical choices in the face of immediate overwhelming circumstances. The changes they conceived and undertook were testimony to their vision as leaders. The sea wall, for example, proved its worth during another severe hurricane that struck Galveston in 1915. Some of the changes instituted in response to the storm lasted well into the twentieth century. Galveston retained the commission form of local government until April 1960, when voters in a referendum abandoned it in favor of the city manager form of governance. Even today, the sea wall and grade raising define Galveston visually and serve as visible reminders of an era when faith in the future, unlimited vision, and positive action worked in concert with each other.

Casey Edward Greene
HEAD OF SPECIAL COLLECTIONS, ROSENBERG LIBRARY
Galveston, Texas

ACKNOWLEDGMENTS

In the course of researching and writing this book, we have incurred a host of debts, many of them scholarly and some of them personal. Three established scholars, John B. Boles, Water Buenger, and David G. McComb, read the manuscript in its entirety and offered valuable advice and helpful encouragement, for which we are extremely grateful. No one can research or write about Galveston or the 1900 Storm without recourse to two important works. David G. McComb's (1986) *Galveston: A History* is still the most detailed general history of the island, and John Edward Weems's (1957, 1980) *Weekend in September* contains a wealth of minutiae about that horrifying weekend from a variety of viewpoints. Weems was fortunate to interview many survivors of the hurricane, and his narrative provides a broad cross section of experience from which we have borrowed.

We have benefited greatly from the assistance of many dedicated archivists. Casey Greene, Anna Peebler, Shelly Henley Kelly, and Julia Dunn make the Galveston and Texas History Center at Rosenberg Library in Galveston an outstanding site for historical research. We are very thankful to Casey Greene for writing the foreword to this book at an especially difficult time. Alice Wygant, Robin Chouanard Munson, and the staff of the Galveston County Historical Museum served above and beyond the call of duty for this project, encouraging book and exhibition as they slowly moved toward completion. Betty Massey, the late Ann Whitby, and the staff and membership of the Galveston Historical Foundation have supported us from the beginning, and we are honored to present this work under their auspices. At the National Archives and Records Administration Southwest Region office in Fort Worth, Texas, Meg Hacker and Pete Scholls exhibited unfailing good humor and great courage in opening untouched cardboard boxes of U.S. Army Corps of Engineering records. Kathy Flynn and Mark Sexton at Peabody Essex Museum in Salem, Massachusetts, demonstrated once again how delightful research at that institution can be. Margaret Schlanke at the Austin Public Library was also very helpful.

Financial support for this work was received from many quarters—testimony, we believe, to the topic's importance for Galveston and the larger community. Early on this effort was perceived to be not only a commemoration but also an attempt to understand the defining event of Galveston, Texas. Funding from the Texas Council for the Humanities, the National Endowment for the Humanities, the Dodge Jones Foundation, the Harris and Eliza Kempner Fund, the Houston Endowment, and Ann Hamilton allowed us to produce a much higher quality product than otherwise would have been possible. Rice University and the University of Houston-Downtown supported our work at every turn, and the staff of the *Journal of Southern History* deserves special thanks.

In writing this book, we wanted to incorporate new materials or sources that may not have been included in earlier works on the storm and recovery. Additional documents concerning the storm have been donated to the Galveston and Texas History Center since Weems wrote his book, and the Galveston County Historical Museum has information of the sea wall and grade raising projects that has only rarely been used. While we made use of many previously published works, we also traveled to less frequently cited archives in search of fresh images and textual accounts. We are grateful to the Library of Congress, which holds a sizable photograph collection related to the storm and Galveston's recovery as well as the Clara Barton Papers; the Southern Historical Collection at the University of North Carolina in Chapel Hill; the National Archives in Fort Worth, Texas; and the Peabody Essex Museum in Salem, Massachusetts; the Austin Public Library; and the Center for American History at the University of Texas at Austin. All provided interesting and valuable items that have enriched this project. We also wish to thank our husbands, Eric Bixel and Al Turner, for the unfailing support and assistance with this project.

Literary collaboration is a delicate affair, and, happily, the stresses of this project were halved rather than doubled by a combined effort. Our previous independent research on Galveston led to a tidy division of labor on this work. Writing about such a catastrophic event contributed perspective to our own lives, as we learned valuable lessons from our survivor subjects. We would like to thank each other for shared wisdom, insight, laughter, and support, and to acknowledge that, in fact, in the end, the 1900 Storm changed our lives as well.

Perhaps our greatest debt is to the survivors, who, by sheer grit, made it through that harrowing night in 1900 and lived to tell about it. Their descriptions of the storm and the willingness of most to stay and rebuild the island have made this story possible. They were the lucky ones. We realize the enormous tragedy of this event; it is for this reason that we dedicate this commemorative volume to the victims and survivors of the 1900 Storm.

GALVESTON AND THE 1900 STORM

~

INTRODUCTION

"A place of unique, sensual beauty"

The appearance of Galveston from the Harbour is singularly dreary.

It is a low flat sandy Island about 30 miles in length & ranging in

breadth from 1 to 2. There is hardly a shrub visible, & in short it

looks like a piece of praiarie [sic] that had quarreled with the main

land & dissolved partnership.

FRANCIS SHERIDAN'S JOURNAL (1839–1840)

GALVESTON ISLAND is one of many barrier islands that parallel the Texas coastline. Waves breaking in shallow water relinquish their loads of sand and silt, gradually building—and re-forming—long, thin ribbons of land that line the Gulf Coast. Rivers and bayous flow into bays behind the strips of sand, and gulf tides help to fill and empty these bights each day through passes between the islands. On the upper Texas coast, the action of currents around the eastern end of Galveston Island—the movement of tides and bay waters through one of these passes—carved a channel, a groove of deep water that allowed most boats and ships access to the safe anchorage on the northern shore of the island.

Located at 29 18′17″ latitude and 94 46′30″ longitude, the island itself is twenty-seven miles long and ranges from one-and-a-half to three miles wide along its length. The island's earliest residents, Karankawa Indians, came to hunt and fish for periods of time but maintained no permanent presence. When explorer Cabeza de Vaca floated ashore in 1528, he was interested in treasure, not economic growth, and made his way through Texas into northern Mexico. Other explorers charted the coastline and noted the island's location; in 1785, on orders from the viceroy of Mexico, Count Bernardo de Galvez, José de Evia mapped the area, calling the bay "Bahia de Galveztowm" [sic]. No permanent settlement appeared until the early nineteenth century when Don Louis Aury, privateer and sometime Mexican revolutionary, arrived on the island, claimed it for Mexico, and established a camp on its eastern end. He used the deep water channel and safe harbor for forays against Spanish shipping and planned an invasion of Mexico to overthrow the government. When Aury abandoned Galveston to lead his revolution, pirate Jean Lafitte moved in, using the camp for his own operations in the western Gulf of Mexico.

More law abiding citizens arrived in Galveston after Lafitte's eviction by the U.S. Navy in 1821. Impresario Stephen F. Austin had received permission from the Mexican government to bring settlers to Texas from the United States, and many of them entered the region through Galveston, which, Austin is reputed to have said, was the best natural harbor he had seen. Under the auspices of Austin and the Mexican government, a small town arose on the eastern tip of the island, and people and vessels began arriving regularly. Galveston was designated a Mexican port of entry in 1825, and a small customs house was constructed in 1830. During the Texas revolution, the Texas Navy was based in the port, and retreating officials of the new republic fled there to escape Mexican forces.

After Texas's successful fight for independence, entrepreneurs moved quickly to capitalize on Galveston's economic potential. Michel B. Menard, through a circuitous series of dealings, gained title to "a league and a labor" (4,604 acres) of land located on the eastern end of the island. Menard and his associates formed the Galveston City Company to sell lots, and the Republic of Texas confirmed the company charter. By the end of 1838, over sixty families claimed Galveston as home, and almost a hundred buildings marked the beginning of this urban center.

Taking advantage of the natural harbor, local businessmen began to build wharves and warehouses to handle ships that called in the young town. Ephraim McLean built the first wharf in 1838, and others followed his example. On February 4, 1854, six investors combined to form the Galveston Wharf Company, a "semi-public company possessing capital stock estimated to be one million dollars." By 1860 seven of the ten existing wharves operated under company ownership. In 1869 a court decree that gave the city one third of the company stock and three seats on the board of directors (although no voting rights) settled a land dispute between the city of Galveston and the Galveston Wharf Company. Port operations were easily the most important factor determining Galveston's economic prosperity, and citizens monitored the company's activities closely.

The port responded vigorously. Until the dredging of channels became commonplace in the late nineteenth and early twentieth centuries, Galveston was the best place on the Texas coast for shipping to move from interior rivers and bayous to the Gulf of Mexico and vice versa, especially before railroads arrived in the region. Cotton, foodstuffs, and other raw materials moved down waterways to Galveston Bay to be loaded on barges or other shallow draft boats for transport to the city of Galveston. There goods could be loaded on ships for export, and small craft picked up imports for transit to the interior. Despite the presence of two pesky sandbars (inner and outer) below water level, currents sweeping around Bolivar Peninsula at the eastern end of the island maintained a channel through the shallow water that permitted entry into Galveston Bay for most vessels at high tide. Ships drawing too much water off-loaded their cargo onto smaller watercraft (lighters) for the trip to the city's wharves and warehouses.

The Civil War disrupted Galveston's growth; much of the population evacuated the town after imposition of the Union blockade. Federal troops maintained a tenuous occupation until Confederates recaptured the city in the battle of Galveston on January 1, 1863. Blockade runners thrived as the U.S. Navy tried to enforce the embargo from offshore. With southern surrender in 1865, the city turned its attention toward expansion once again.

When army engineers conducted the first surveys of the region in the 1850s, they found common features among all the harbor entrances along the Texas coast. On either side of each pass, the southern headland—a point of land extending outward into the water—extended farther into the Gulf than its northern counterpart. Easterly winds combined with currents to cause land located on the southern side of each pass to gradually wear away. Over time, this activity was easily discernible on the eastern end of Galveston, where the end of the island shifted westward almost twelve hundred yards from 1841 until 1870. Besides changing the topography, the

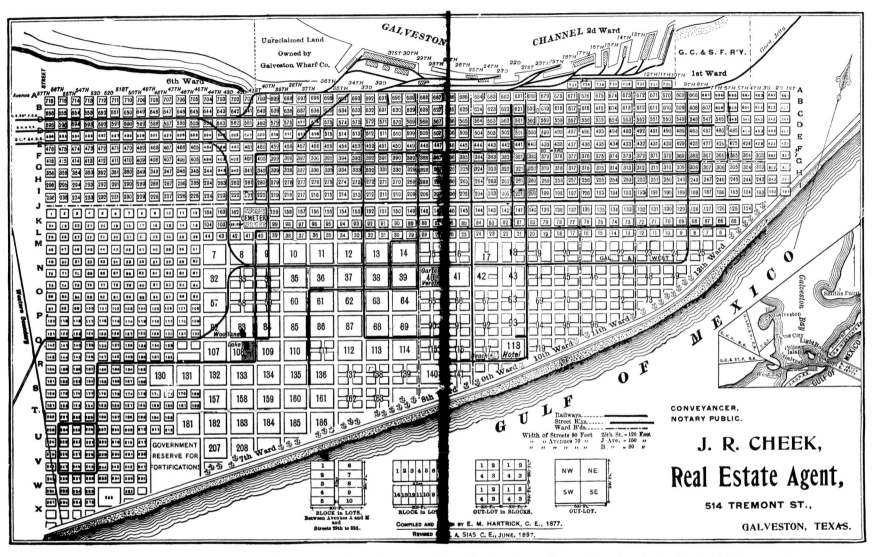

FIGURE INT.1: Galveston in 1900. This city directory map shows the densely packed eastern end of Galveston Island. From the port on its northern side to its southern beachfront, homes and businesses flourished in the coastal city. Commercial activity centered around the port, where large buildings fanned outward from the piers that lined the waterfront. No wider than three miles anywhere along its length, the island narrowed considerably on its eastern end; someone standing at 25th Street and Broadway could see ships glide down the channel or waves break upon the beach depending on which direction he or she glanced. (Courtesy Rosenberg Library, Galveston, Texas.)

erosion also resulted in the deviation of the channel and the gradual increase in the height of the inner bar at the mouth of the harbor. By the 1850s water over the inner bar rarely reached fifteen feet.

Even before the Civil War, the cities of Galveston and Houston developed a serious economic rivalry. Placement of new rail lines and Houston's growth during the conflict threatened Galveston's economic position in the state and region, so the island city worked even harder to secure and maintain its dominance. Depth of water over the bars was an ongoing concern, especially as ships became larger and as the natural forces mentioned above changed the depth, course, and shape of the channel. Every Sunday the newspaper published readings of the "depth of water on Galveston's outer bar," and local leaders lobbied governmental officials for state or federal money for harbor improvements. In 1881 Galveston leaders formed the "Committee on Deep Water," which was composed of prominent business leaders and charged with protecting the port's interests in various state and national circles. What became known as the Deep Water Committee also worked to secure support for deepening the channel either by dredging or by constructing jetties to work against the natural buildup of the sandbars near the harbor entrance. The committee's efforts increased after members saw that scouring action caused by man-made jetties eroded the sandbars that were obstructing the mouth of the Mississippi River. City leaders believed that constructing similar jetties around the Galveston channel would wear away the bars that hampered entrance to the port. By 1889 the federal government acknowledged the need to support development of a single deep harbor west of New Orleans. In December of that year, U.S. Army engineers determined that Galveston was the best site for that port, and Congress began to appropriate funds for harbor work. By 1897 northern and southern jetties were completed, and on May 16, 1897, the *Belgian King* crossed the outer bar drawing 24 feet, 7 inches, a marked increase over earlier depths.

Regular steamship service between Galveston and other Gulf and Atlantic coast cities began in 1838, and by 1899 the city boasted service that included fourteen direct steamship lines to Europe, three lines to Cuba, one line to Mexico, and two lines servicing Japan and the Far East. The port took pride in "wharves less than three miles from the sea." For the year 1899, the Galveston port ranked second in the country in cotton exports, third in wheat, sixth in cattle, seventh in corn, and thirteenth in flour. The city could claim one of the largest flour mills in the state, the only cotton bagging mill south of St. Louis, a cotton mill, rope and twine mills, breweries, and plants manufacturing crackers, pickles, and vinegar. Beyond that, Galveston was the first city in the state with electricity, gas lights, and telephones.

Galveston was a seaport, and its population and lifestyle reflected the arrival and departure of ships and passengers from all parts of the globe. Merchant seamen frequented the city's taverns and "sailortown," taking advantage of the traditional port pleasures with which Galveston abounded. The city had the dubious distinction of claiming more saloons (489) than any city of comparable size and more than any other Gulf port—including New Orleans—as well as around fifty houses of prostitution. Immigrants arrived on a regular basis from the 1850s onward; a few remained on the island, but more frequently they moved to towns in the interior of the state or joined relatives elsewhere in the region. After the Civil War, enterprising businessmen established themselves in the banking, shipping, jobbing, and retail operations that began to flourish.

Galveston's population was predominantly of European extraction in 1899; 40 percent of islanders cited roots in England, Germany, Ireland, or France. African Americans made up about 20 percent of the island's residents, and they were a group with an educated and active middle class and strong presence among the professions and the skilled labor force on the docks. Italians, eastern Europeans, and a relatively small number of people of Hispanic descent composed the rest of the census. Galveston was surprisingly Catholic for a southern city, and the annual Mardi Gras celebration, begun in 1867, marked a high point on the island social calendar. Besides Catholic parishes, there were thirty-nine Protestant and

Jewish congregations. Baptists dominated (eight black and four white congregations), with Methodists (four black, four white), Episcopalians (one black, three white), Presbyterian (four), and Lutheran (three) churches fulfilling the bulk of the spiritual needs of the city. Two Jewish synagogues and groups of Disciples of Christ, Christian Scientists, Swedenborgians, and Spiritualists also thrived. Most denominations sponsored women's or youth groups, and many supported charitable institutions within the community.

Galveston was also a center of wealth and culture. The "season" ran from November to April, and residents could be busy from dawn to dusk. The city welcomed Edwin Booth, Lily Langtry, Sarah Bernhardt, and even Buffalo Bill to its theaters and opera houses. The Galveston Lyceum addressed important issues of the day; the Galveston Historical Society sought to preserve Texas history; and numerous musicals, concerts, and picnics entertained the population. The Garten Verein was the site of picnics, concerts, and dances, and several beer gardens catered to the German population. Woolam's Lake was another popular location for boating and parties.

There were bicycle races at the velodrome, sailboat races, and rowing contests. Baseball and boxing found audiences on the island after Reconstruction. Black heavyweight champion Jack Johnson was born in Galveston and worked on the docks before gaining fame in the ring.

John W. Thomason Jr. was one of the island's summer visitors as more and more Texans decided to spend their vacations on the seashore. Writing years later, he explained:

it was the custom of gentlefolk from the upcountry towns to summer at Galveston. The Gulf breeze cooled the city at nightfall; one of the most beautiful beaches in the world offered delightful surf-bathing; and you saw everybody there in the afternoons, bathing, promenading or driving in carriages on the smooth, crisp sands. There were ample hotels providing luxurious accommodations for the wealthy, and a score of lesser hostelries invited the more prudent spenders. Bettison's Pier on the north jetty was an unrivalled fishing establishment: Murdock's Restaurant over the surf a splendid place to eat and to watch the waves. As to the city, it was lovely: its flat white buildings stood up from the water with the thin aspect of unreality; its streets were lined with oleanders; its lawns shaded by numerous palm trees; its verandas deep and draped with vines.

Local benefactors funded parks and charities, and a Swiss immigrant, Henry Rosenberg, provided four hundred thousand dollars in his will for the construction of a public library. In addition, Rosenberg eased life for Galvestonians in a very practical way. Besides serving on many charitable boards and committees, through a bequest at his death he funded seventeen public water fountains that provided clean water for man and beast at various locations throughout the city.

Historian David G. McComb summarizes Galveston's position at the turn of the century:

the Island City was the most advanced and sophisticated in Texas. True, it had begun to slip. . . . Galveston trailed Houston, Dallas, and San Antonio [in population]. It would never catch up, but at the time this fact was but dimly grasped. Galveston still was the most important port, it was the first to have telephones and electricity, it had the best newspapers and theater, it had the greatest variety of sports, it had the most individual wealth and the most advanced architecture, and it was a place of unique, sensual beauty which every visitor could feel.

Galveston's port was her lifeblood, but the coastal position that gave her wealth carried risk as well. Most of the city was barely above high tide level; and when tides were unusually high, many streets and alleys flooded. The highest elevation on the island—just under nine feet—was Broadway, the wide boulevard that ran east to west and bisected the city. From there the city sloped southward toward the Gulf of Mexico and northward toward the bay and port. Western parts of the town were even lower, and areas of

FIGURES INT.2, INT.3: Galveston's Garten Verein was the city's leading German social club in the late nineteenth century. In 1876, bankruptcy prompted financier Robert Mills to sell his five-acre homestead to the club, which then converted the Mills's house into a clubhouse and commissioned extensive landscaping and the construction of bowling alleys, tennis courts, and croquet grounds. The park was an extremely popular gathering place for elites and members of the city's German population. The dancing pavilion, shown in FIG. INT.2, was constructed in 1879–1880.

The park and dancing pavilion offered food and music during the summer with a full schedule of concerts and picnics. Young and old gathered at the venerable establishment; it was the site of many a romantic rendezvous along with hearty meals, songfests, bowling matches, and dances. Purchased by Stanley Kempner in 1923, the park was donated to the city. In 1998, after a full restoration and renovation, the Garten Verein continues to anchor Kempner Park and host weddings and parties. (Courtesy Rosenberg Library, Galveston, Texas.)

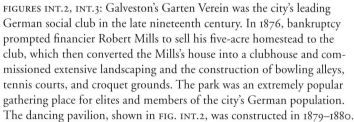

FIGURE INT.4: Successful politician, lawyer, and investor Colonel Walter Gresham commissioned architect Nicholas Clayton to design an extravagant house for the colonel and his family during the competitive mansion-building boom along Broadway. The resulting four-story, gabled, towered, stone mansion was finished in 1892 and still presides at the corner of Broadway and 14th Street. In 1923 the house was purchased by the Roman Catholic diocese as housing for Bishop Christopher Byrne, but in 1963, thirteen years after the bishop's death, the house was opened by the diocese as a museum. (Courtesy Rosenberg Library, Galveston, Texas.)

FIGURE INT.5: The first of the Broadway palaces, Ashton Villa was built in 1859 by hardware magnate and banker J. M. Brown. The Browns had the advantage of all the modern conveniences: gas lighting and heating, indoor plumbing, and closets. The Browns welcomed former president Ulysses S. Grant and his wife in March 1880 while the Grants were on their world tour. Modified over the years, the house has been operated by the Galveston Historical Foundation as a house museum since 1974. (Courtesy Rosenberg Library, Galveston, Texas.)

FIGURE INT.6: Swiss philanthropist Henry Rosenberg bequeathed seventeen fountains to the City of Galveston for the provision of drinking water to residents and their horses and dogs. Located throughout the city, most of the fountains were destroyed or dismantled by the mid-twentieth century. Since 1965, ten surviving structures have been reassembled and reinstalled, the most elaborate currently located at the corner of 21st Street and Postoffice Street, near the 1894 Grand Opera House. (Courtesy Rosenberg Library, Galveston, Texas.)

marsh alternated with patches of higher ground. When tropical weather systems with their attendant winds, rain, and higher tides approached the island, residents learned to seek shelter until the bad weather passed and waters receded. Local records noted particularly bad storms in 1834, 1837, 1847, 1854, 1867, 1875, and 1886. Storms in 1875 and 1886 wiped out the town of Indianola, which was located on Matagorda Bay about one hundred miles south of Galveston, but islanders ignored that object lesson and continued to view occasional "overflows" quite casually.

Local residents and entrepreneurs seemed oblivious to the threat posed by Gulf waters. As Galveston's seashore began attracting visitors, islanders removed indigenous groupings of salt cedar trees to improve access to the beach, which further eased the water's way into low-lying areas. In addition, as island development moved westward, builders took sand from the dunes to fill in shallow areas upon which to build. By the late nineteenth century, the trees and dunes—natural barriers protecting the island's interior—no longer impeded waves from the Gulf.

The city's problem was compounded by its openness to flooding from the bay side of the island. Besides the daily tidal rise, water from Galveston Bay rose even more whenever there was a strong wind from the north or when rising rivers flooded into the bay; the city faced high-water dangers on two sides. Though aware of these threats, prominent businessmen and politicians were reluctant to commit the amount of funding that would be necessary to achieve any level of protection for the city or to stop activities—the removal of trees and dune sand—believed to encourage economic growth. Discussion of building a sea wall came and went with each storm season; and every time Galveston escaped without serious damage, calls for such safeguards faded.

The year 1900 began promisingly for Galveston. The Spanish-American War was over, and shipping traffic resumed its normal level. On January 16, 1900, C. P. Huntington confirmed the purchase of the Galveston, Houston, and Henderson Railroad and its integration into the larger Southern Pacific rail system. Exports still greatly exceeded imports in port traffic, but the rapid growth of

Texas and the upper coast meant increases in arriving goods as well.

In the spring, Galvestonians completed the Texas Heroes Monument, a magnificent edifice at the intersection of 25th Street and Broadway, that celebrated Texas's success at the battle of San Jacinto and the subsequent victory for Texas independence. The statue had

FIGURES INT.7, INT.8: Sculpted by Louis Amateis, the Texas Heroes Monument was one of the bequests of Henry Rosenberg. The commission and installation of monumental civic art was one of the primary components of the City Beautiful movement that flourished at the turn of the century. Trustees of the Rosenberg estate hired the Washington, D.C.,

based sculptor to create the seventy-two-foot-high bronze and granite monument commemorating those who fought in the Texas Revolution. Two seated figures at the base of the monument signify Defiance (facing east) and Peace (facing west). Portraits of Texas heroes Stephen F. Austin and Sam Houston are also incorporated into the work as well as bronze relief sections depicting events at Goliad, the Alamo, and San Jacinto. The monument was dedicated by Governor Joseph D. Sayers on San Jacinto Day, April 21, 1900, five months before the hurricane. (Courtesy Rosenberg Library, Galveston, Texas.)

been part of the bequest of Henry Rosenberg, and the Sidney Sherman chapter of the Daughters of the Republic of Texas supervised its construction. It was dedicated on April 21, 1900—the anniversary of the battle of San Jacinto—and celebrated with a long parade and ceremony, the occasion marked by many speeches and much band music.

For most of the country the year began January 1, but for large portions of Galveston, the calendar began on September 1, when cotton season opened. Each September the Galveston *Daily News* acknowledged the event with a large feature devoted to an annual business report of "the trade and commerce of the Port of Galveston." The 1900–1901 season was no exception, and economic forecasters were overwhelmingly optimistic. Galveston had surpassed New Orleans to become the top cotton port in the nation, and during 1899 had moved to second place (after New York) in wheat exports. Transport problems caused by the Spanish-American War were over, and while the troublesome Boers in South Africa affected British ships and shipping, Galveston leaders watched for an expansion in traffic through the port as the year progressed.

For the first week of September, the front page of the newspaper reported the ongoing Boxer Rebellion in China and assorted European adventures. The 1900 presidential race was shaping up, and the *Daily News* dutifully recounted speeches by candidates William McKinley and William Jennings Bryan. The status of cotton on the world market was reported on a daily basis, and the decision by Lancashire spinners whether to buy concerned many in the Gulf port. Each Sunday the paper listed the depth of water over Galveston's outer bar for the previous week. On Tuesday, September 5, the *Daily News* described the Labor Day parade of the previous afternoon, and local unions were commended for their "fine showing in the procession." The writer commented that "there seemed to be more good humor, snap and ginger about yesterday's parade than any turnout for the past several years." Peightal and Booth, contracting tinners, received first prize for their float, which

was in the shape of a star on either side of the float, and ornamented with fancy tin work. cornice [sic] worker's furnaces, tinners' tools, and decorative work were placed so as to form a pleasing display. . . . A huge, well fashioned eagle, all in tinwork, was perched aloft."

The carpenter's union and the screwmen's benevolent association also received prizes.

Elsewhere in the paper that Tuesday, a tropical disturbance was noted to be "moving northward over western Cuba." Eastbound vessels were advised to expect high winds over the eastern Gulf and Florida coast.

As evidenced by the expansive Labor Day celebration, Galveston had a large and active working class. In March 1857, island printers organized the first permanent labor union in Texas to work for higher wages; by 1860 they had become affiliated with the national group and became Local 28. Before the outbreak of the Civil War, a carpenters' union had been formed as well, Carpenters Local No. 7, and shortly after the Civil War, screwmen on the docks banded together in the Screwmen's Benevolent Association (S.B.A.), a mutual aid society that provided wages during sickness, death benefits, and health care for members. Screwmen were the aristocracy of dockworkers; working in gangs of five, they loaded ships with cotton. Efficiently stowing cotton in ships' holds was their special craft. Using two-hundred-pound jackscrews, they squeezed the loosely packed bales within the hold so that more cotton could be forced into the space. Before the advent of cotton compresses, screwmen could increase a cargo by 10 to 20 percent through their skill at compacting the bales. Black screwmen, led by Norris Wright Cuney, organized as well, forming the Negro Screwmen's Benevolent Association in 1876 and in 1879 the Cotton Jammers' Association. Black cooks, waiters, and barbers also organized unions in the city.

By the 1870s over a dozen nationally affiliated unions participated in the civic life of the island, and Galveston locals supported national labor actions in the 1880s and 1890s. Begun as mutual aid

FIGURE INT.9: Galvestonians celebrated each Labor Day with an elaborate parade that featured floats constructed by the city's locals. (Courtesy Rosenberg Library, Galveston, Texas.)

societies, most of the organizations gradually assumed responsibility for negotiations concerning wages and working conditions. By 1900 Galveston labor groups actively participated in local politics as well, supporting candidates from within their social class and other politicians whose positions were deemed pro-labor. The Galveston *Journal* claimed to be the "Official Organ of Labor Unions and Central Bodies of Galveston" in 1899, and its editor, William V. McConn, safeguarded workers' interests through a sharp eye on city leaders. African American labor concerns were a focus of the black-owned and operated *City Times*.

In 1894 representatives from county locals formed the Galveston Labor Council, which claimed three thousand members by 1899. Twenty-nine labor organizations were listed in the 1901 city directory. The Cigar Makers Union claimed fifteen members, while the island's largest union, the Screwman's Benevolent Association, recorded six hundred. Not unexpectedly, the most prominent associations were composed of those involved in transportation industries: waterfront workers, railroad employees, streetcar operators, and others involved in such businesses. Galveston was also home to an assortment of urban unions: barbers, musicians, retail clerks, cooks and waiters, and others employed in city service areas as well as a wide variety of building trades groups. For the most part, business and labor interests coincided; all were interested in promoting a positive economic climate, the port, and continued growth on the island.

Life on a sandbar attracted many people. The island was a sensuous place with balmy soft breezes, the rhythmic cadence of breakers on the beach, and lush tropical foliage; an economic center providing financial, commercial, and transportation services for the region; a cosmopolitan city with grand houses, restaurants, hotels, entertainments; and a place with an always fluctuating population of wealthy, interesting, powerful people. It was also a city completely oblivious of its imminent destruction.

Most writing about the 1900 Storm falls into two categories. In the months immediately after the storm, a wide variety of sensa-

tionalist accounts were published that capitalized on the death and damage visited upon the city. As the city recovered, Clarence Ousley, in conjunction with local leaders, produced *Galveston in 1900*, a book that was a direct rejoinder to the wildly exaggerated accounts that were flooding the market. In it, he sought to separate fact from grandly embroidered rumor and fiction, and proceeds from Ousley's book went to support the restoration of the public schools. Since the disaster, a few works for the general public have appeared based upon first-person accounts of experiences during the storm. In articles for the popular press, some writers have looked at the institution of the commission government, the construction of the sea wall, or the grade raising. A few professional historians have addressed narrow, specific aspects of the hurricane or recovery in dissertations or academic monographs, but no single general or popular work has taken a long view of the event, examining the storm and the years afterward to explore the changes wrought by the disaster and the response to it. The centennial of the storm, September 8, 2000, seemed the perfect time to present not only an account of the hurricane but also a discussion of its short- and long-term consequences—what happened after sunrise, September 9, 1900.

To understand the hurricane as a catastrophic weather event through the accounts of its survivors is only part of the story. How Galveston responded to the storm—how decisions about relief, leadership, recovery, and reconstruction were made and how they affected island residents—is the rest of the tale and the portion most useful in understanding the city that Galveston became after September 1900. What follows is both a straightforward description of events and an interpretation of what those events meant for Galvestonians and, in some cases, the rest of the country. The first chapter follows a broad cross section of individuals and groups through the terror of that night and documents the wide range of experiences recounted by survivors. Relief efforts immediately after the storm are outlined in the second chapter. Decisions made and actions taken by city government, the Central Relief Committee,

African American leaders, and the Women's Health Protective Association are discussed, and the role of relief agencies—especially the Red Cross—through the first year after the storm is explained. Long-term changes prompted by the storm are the subject of the third chapter, which outlines the rationale behind instituting the commission form of government and details the development and implementation of plans for the sea wall and grade raising. The fourth chapter examines more closely the ramifications of some of these decisions—how changes in government and the experiences of storm recovery and reconstruction created new business opportunities, fostered new political actors, and led to racial and social changes not usually associated with national disasters.

The most difficult aspect of reconstructing events of the storm and recovery centers around the availability of African American sources. Black Galvestonians made up one fifth of the population and had a strong public presence in the city prior to 1900, but many records revealing this were destroyed in the storm. The leadership of Norris Wright Cuney was the most visible evidence of black participation in political and economic life after the Civil War. Cuney was a Republican, former state representative, city alderman, and successful businessman. Appointed collector of customs for the district of Texas in 1889 by President Benjamin Harrison, he so impressed the white elite of Galveston that they included him in discussions concerning the city's future and afforded him a level of respect rarely seen in the late nineteenth-century South. His involvement in city boards, commissions, labor negotiations, and elections assured the black community a voice in local politics. His death in 1898 was a serious blow. No other single black leader had the political and economic clout of Cuney. For a variety of reasons, the homes and businesses of black Galvestonians were destroyed in disproportionate numbers in the 1900 hurricane and irreplaceable records of black institutions—churches, women's groups, schools, and others—were lost as well. A few black newspapers are available on microfilm; some letters, personal accounts, and manuscript records may be gleaned from larger collections,

but there is a dearth of information about what it was like to be black in Galveston from 1900 to 1915.

We are both historians, and in previous work involving Galveston topics, we were struck by the overwhelming importance of the storm for not only Galveston or Texas history but also for the larger story of American disaster relief, Progressivism, municipal reform, and modern technological development. If Galveston, Texas, appears in history texts, it is in conjunction with the implementation of the commission form of government, a direct outgrowth of storm recovery. Many leaders of the Texas and national woman suffrage movements came from the ranks of the Women's Health Protective Association, a group that gained prominence, political authority, and practical organizational experience in the aftermath of the storm. Constructing the sea wall and raising the island grade remain major feats of civil engineering with ramifications for coastal development that are only beginning to be understood. And the storm remains the worst natural disaster in terms of lives lost ever to strike North America.

Along with ruin came opportunity, and community leaders made choices that set the tone for all that would come later. While we may applaud those decisions, we must also understand that they carried with them a wide range of consequences, not all of them positive. Accepting the commission form of government meant more efficient operation of local administrations, but it also eliminated representation for large portions of the electorate. Women received power and authority from the prevailing leadership as black men and the white working class lost influence, and political actions taken after the storm eased the way for Galveston to impose sanctions of the Jim Crow South on the city's black population. The sea wall and grade raising have protected the island, but the wall's construction created an erosion process that wears away the beaches. Maintaining the wall *and* island beaches—and the tourism that they bring—requires constant and expensive maintenance.

The dictionary defines "catalyst" as "a substance . . . that enables a chemical reaction to proceed at a usually faster rate or under different conditions . . . than otherwise possible" or as "an agent that provokes or speeds significant change or action." For Galveston, the 1900 hurricane was unquestionably a catastrophe—but it was also a catalyst. The hurricane that devastated the island brought enormous social, political, and economic upheaval. Even the geography changed. The storm was a disaster of extraordinary magnitude, and in its aftermath, leaders made decisions that not only shaped the city's recovery but also determined in many ways the outline of its urban future. From September 8, 1900, until

August 17, 1915, Galveston remade itself as a southern city. Citizens labored mightily to regain an economic position fast slipping away and to persuade outsiders that such devastation would never be repeated. To emerge from the wreckage on September 9, 1900, was to enter a new world. This book and its accompanying exhibition seek to understand that world and its inhabitants, their responses to the tragedy around them, and their reconstruction of a place and way of life lost to the winds and waves on that weekend in September.

CHAPTER ONE

"A thousand little devils, shrieking and whistling"

September 8, 1900

I have passed through the most trying, horrible thing in my life.

God knows that on Saturday night at 9 o'clock I had given up all

hopes of ever seeing the light of day and my prayers were on my lips

asking God to take care of you and the little darling there at home

as it seemed that I would be floating with the thousand poor dead

bodies out in the streets at any moment.

CHARLES LAW TO HIS WIFE, SEPTEMBER 12, 1900

"ANOTHER OVERFLOW" was the way many Galvestonians described the inconvenience of high water on the morning of September 8, 1900. Given the nearby Gulf of Mexico and generally low profile of the island, knee-deep water in yards and along alleys was not all that unusual in the community. Periodically, storms or particularly high tides forced water up into the streets and people's yards. It was a nuisance, but easy enough to bear. Most Galveston buildings were raised—built on piers or pilings expressly to prevent the encroachment of rising water. What people did not understand was that today, September 8, 1900, the unusually high—and rising—tides were harbingers of much worse to come.

Isaac Monroe Cline and his brother Joseph noted the rather strange weather pattern and surveyed the skies and measured winds for clues to the approaching conditions. Isaac Cline was the local forecast official for the Galveston Weather Bureau and section director for its parent, the U.S. Weather Bureau. He had established the Texas section of the U.S. Weather Service in 1889 and was heavily involved in its expansion, the application of scientific methods to weather forecasting and climatology, and the upgrading of personnel at bureau offices. His brother, Joseph L. Cline, was the Galveston bureau's chief clerk. A third weather observer, John Blagden, temporarily replaced a member of the office who was taking a three-month leave. These men weighed information from Washington against their local observations and determined that something—most likely a tropical cyclone—was taking aim at the island.

Weather forecasting, especially the type that could predict tropi-

FIGURE 1.1: Isaac Monroe Cline, head of the weather bureau in Galveston. Cline posted warnings as he received them from the U.S. Weather Bureau in Washington, but hurricane warning and prediction was in its infancy in 1900. Cline lost his wife in the storm, and both he and his brother were hospitalized for injuries. Cline left Galveston for New Orleans in 1901, where he worked for the weather service until his retirement in 1935. (Photo from *Storms, Floods and Sunshine: A Book of Memoirs* by Isaac Monroe Cline © 1945; used by permission of the licenser, Pelican Publishing Company, Inc.)

cal storm movement, was in its infancy. Connected by telephone and telegraph to other bureau offices and Washington, D.C., Cline and the Galveston bureau both sent and received forecasting messages each day, but following a storm track over water, out at sea, was as yet impossible. Not until the invention of ship-to-shore communication would forecasters have information about weather systems from ships at sea. The first such communication occurred in 1905, but nothing of this sort was available to the Clines. Coastal weather bureaus relied upon reports from other land-based observers. As early as Tuesday, September 4, 1900, reports from the Washington bureau noted that "[t]he influence of the tropical storm now extends over Cuba and the northwest Caribbean Sea. It has thus far developed but little force, but has caused torrential rains at many places . . . For the present this storm will probably cause nothing more severe than strong northeasterly winds from the Caribbean Sea northward over the south Atlantic . . ." On Thursday, the bureau was reporting that "[t]he tropical storm is central this morning north of Key West. It has increased somewhat in energy and caused severe northeast gales over portions of southern Florida. . . . Hurricane warnings are displayed from Cedar Keys to Savannah; storm warnings from Charleston to Kitty Hawk and from Pensacola to New Orleans." By Friday, September 7, the news was increasingly worrisome. The 8:00 A.M. (EST) bulletin placed the storm "central this morning in the Gulf of Mexico south of Louisiana . . . moving slowly northwestward. . . . Storm warnings are displayed from Pensacola to Galveston."

The Cline brothers and Blagden compared their observations with information they were receiving from Washington and other stations. No ship reports from arriving vessels supplemented bureau station readings, and the weather officials became increasingly troubled. Cline had been posting the storm warnings since the previous Tuesday, and he watched the skies nervously. When warnings were extended to Galveston on Friday, Cline hoisted the appropriate flags atop the Levy Building, at the corner of 23rd Street (Tremont) and Avenue D (Market), the location of the weather bureau. The traditional signal—a red flag with a black square in the center—alerted islanders to the approach of a dangerous weather system. The white pennant flown above the red flag indicated that winds would come from the northwest.

Part of the problem was that the usual warning signs were not present. A "brick-dust sky was not in evidence to the smallest degree," wrote Cline in a special report after the storm, and in his autobiography he explained that "neither the barometer, nor the winds were telling me." Only the steadily rising tide, despite winds from the north against it, warned of the approaching hurricane.

Galveston's police chief, Edwin N. Ketchum, mentioned the storm warning to his family at dinner Friday night. The Ketchums lived on the west side of the city, in a large house that had been built by one of Galveston's founders, Michel B. Menard. Winds were still light, so the chief postponed precautions; every indication was that the storm would be a mild one.

Joseph Cline awoke from a restless sleep around 4:00 A.M. Saturday morning to find the tide in his yard. Joseph lived with his brother's family in a house about four blocks from the beach. He quickly woke Isaac, and the two conferred about what was to be done. By 5:00 A.M. Isaac Cline was on the beach, checking the height of the tide and time between swells while Joseph went to the office. They met there later, checked the instruments (the barometer had fallen only one tenth of an inch since the previous night), and Isaac returned to the shoreline. Rain poured by midmorning; both Clines were sure a bad storm was coming. On his second trip to the beach, Isaac Cline drove his buggy along the sand, warning visitors to leave the island. He told residents who lived within three blocks of the water to seek higher ground, to move into stronger buildings nearer the city center. Ebb and flow of the rising tides would destroy buildings on the Gulf side of the island as the city was slowly but surely inundated. Later he sent a telegram to Washington:

Unusually heavy swells from southeast, intervals one to five minutes overflowing low places south portion of city three to four blocks from beach. Such high water with opposing winds never observed previously.

Throughout the day, either Joseph Cline or John Blagden manned the telephone to answer questions and to warn callers of the serious storm threatening the island. By early afternoon Isaac Cline determined that a special report should be sent to Washington. While Joseph checked the instruments on top of the Levy Building, Isaac drove first to the bay side of the island and then back to the beach. What he saw did not allay any fears. "Gulf rising, water cover [sic] streets of about half city," he reported to his brother Joseph. He added that the city was going underwater, a great many lives might be lost, and relief efforts would probably be necessary. Joseph's instrument readings offered no consolation. The rain gauge had already blown away; the wind was from the northeast at forty-two miles per hour; the barometer continued to drop; and a heavy rain was falling.

Isaac Cline set out for home while Joseph waded through the water to the telegraph office to send the message to Washington. Finding that the wires were down, he returned to the weather office and tried the telephone. Joseph asked for the Houston Western Union Office. One long distance line remained to connect Galveston with the rest of the world; thousands of calls were ahead of his. Using all of the federal clout that he could muster, Cline convinced the manager, Tom Powell, to give him the line. Joseph sent the message, and shortly after 3:00 P.M. on Saturday afternoon, the line went dead.

Just as modern coastal residents vary in their responses to storm warnings, so did turn-of-the-century Galvestonians. "Overflows" were nothing new to islanders, and, other than the rising water, the weather early Saturday morning seemed perfectly agreeable. Years after the event, storm survivors related various reactions to the warnings. James Monroe Fendley commented that "the storm was forecast by the Weather Bureau, but we had had storms before, and most people considered themselves safe in their own houses." "True, the weather man foretold bad weather & urged precaution," recalled Henry M. Wortham years later, "and while hundreds perhaps thousands thought of the prediction very few heeded the danger signals." "Mama didn't want to leave. She'd been through it before and wasn't worried. It never had been that bad," remembered Jennie Karbowski in 1988. Louisa Christine Rollfing recalled that "no one was alarmed more than at any other time when we heard these reports. Everybody went about their business in the same way as on any other Saturday."

For most people, Saturday was a workday, and they were busy attending to their employment. Until Isaac Cline implored beachgoers to seek higher ground, few took the warnings seriously. Joseph Cline and Blagden entreated those who called or visited the bureau office to seek safe shelter away from the wind and tides, but for many the warnings came too late.

Isaac H. ("Ike") Kempner went downtown that Saturday for a business meeting with Joseph A. Kemp and Henry Sayles. The men were in town to discuss irrigation plans for land in Wichita County. Sayles was a lawyer from Abilene, and Kemp was from Wichita Falls; they were interested in damming a creek. After the meeting, Kempner noticed the worsening weather and climbed into his buggy for the trip home; the other two men went to the Union Passenger station, intending to catch the next train out of the city. A growing number of people were gathering at the station, many of them hoping to get out of town before the worst of the storm, but ticket sellers had stopped selling by noon. Water covered tracks onto the island, and no trains were running.

The last train left Galveston around 9:00 A.M. the morning of the 8th, bound for Houston. Passengers on the regularly scheduled train from Houston, which usually left that city at 9:45 A.M., arrived on the island around 1:00 P.M. A washed-out section of track required riders to transfer to a Galveston, Houston, and Henderson relief train sent from the island, and riders made a slow trip into the city with railroad workers walking ahead of the engine to clear debris from the track. Passengers approaching from Beaumont (to the east of the city) shortly before noon expected to take a launch across the bay for the last few miles, but the horrible weather made that impossible. The train tried to return to Beaumont, but rising water forced passengers and crew to take refuge

with the Port Bolivar lighthouse keeper, H. C. Claiborne, and his family.

Throughout the afternoon, Galveston residents came to terms with Cline's warnings and readied for a blow. Most people within a few blocks of the shore did go to higher ground, and thousands of lives were saved in this way. The Friday afternoon before, schoolteacher Daisy Thorne had decided not to go to the beach because of the ugly brown water and waves crashing on shore. Instead, she remained in her apartment on the northwest corner of Broadway and 6th Street where she lived with her mother, sister, brother, and aunt in number 5, Lucas Terrace, a large three-story brick apartment building. Saturday morning the water had already reached the section of Broadway near Lucas Terrace. Thorne took photographs of the pounding surf from the building's front porch as others walked toward the beach for a better look. Water had covered that end of Broadway for hours, but she wasn't worried. Overflows were part of life in Galveston, and she had played in them as a child. Some neighbors arrived at the Thornes's, afraid to stay in their less substantial dwellings, and Daisy's mother welcomed them with coffee and biscuits.

Another Galveston resident, Walter Grover, also tried to carry on as usual. He walked to the real estate office downtown where he worked, noting the massive waves breaking on the beach not far away, and stayed in his office until noon. After a meal at the Elite Restaurant—where he watched the wind batter nearby buildings—he walked to the wharves, which were almost under water. When he returned to the office, Grover met John Adriance, and the two braved the worsening weather in a buggy bound for Grover's house. At home, Grover's sister wanted to venture out for a glimpse of the storm's effects. They attempted to drive the buggy toward the beach, but conditions threatened horse, carriage, and passengers. After taking his sister home, Grover and Adriance went a few blocks to the Adriance home in order to stable the horse. Not yet convinced of the storm's severity, the two men left to explore on foot.

FIGURE 1.2: Lucas Terrace apartments, after the hurricane. Located near the beach at 6th Street and Market, these apartments bore the brunt of the hurricane. Over fifty people died in the structure; perhaps more surprisingly, twenty-two people survived. Daisy Thorne's fiancé, Dr. Joe Gilbert, rushed to the island after the storm, fearful for his intended wife. They were married on September 13 at Grace Episcopal Church, most likely the first wedding after the hurricane. When the couple left for Austin the next day, Daisy took her last remaining cat—the only one to survive the 1900 Storm. (Courtesy Prints and Photographs Division, Library of Congress, Washington, D.C.)

Mrs. Charles Vidor, mother of future filmmaker King Vidor, packed up King and two young visitors from Fort Worth to go to the beach to see the breakers. Years later, Vidor wrote a story for *Esquire* magazine, "Southern Storm," in which he used the experience:

As we looked up the sandy street the mile to the sea, I could see the waves crash against the streetcar trestle, then shoot into the air as high as the telephone poles. Higher. My mother didn't speak as we watched three or four waves. I was only five then, but I remember now that it seemed as if we were in a bowl looking up toward the level of the sea. As we stood there in the sandy street, my mother and I, I wanted to take my mother's hand and hurry her away. I felt as if the sea was going to break over the edge of the bowl and come pouring down upon us.

Vidor's mother recalled a large bathhouse being pounded by the surf. When it began to rain, the woman and three boys took refuge in the nearby home of George W. Boschke on 23rd Street and Avenue N. Boschke was a Southern Pacific Railroad official and host to the Fort Worth visitors.

Some islanders were even less prepared. Phillip Gordie (P. G.) Tipp left town on Wednesday, September 5, by sailboat with two other men—Will Jay and Christ Meyers—to fish and hunt in West Galveston Bay. Equipped with provisions for several days and with five fish cars to hold the catch, they sailed briskly through the bay and set anchors in the mouth of Taylor's Bayou. That night they lit flounder torches and split up to catch fish. Tipp had great success until the small shell island he was working around was completely covered by water. He returned to the boat, deposited his fish in the first fish car, and made coffee in the cabin while he waited for his friends.

On Thursday morning the fishermen tried to return to Galveston before the bad weather turned worse, but they were forced to return to the bayou. They anchored again, fixed dinner, played cards, and hoped the storm would pass. All day Friday they continued to wait while the skies darkened, the water rose, and the wind howled. Tipp described the night:

The wind got way up, and the sea just whipped the boat all evening, and we sat wondering all kinds of things. At midnight it finally happened. The wind just picked us up off the top of a wave and slung us down on the island, upside down. All hell broke loose, none of us was hurt, just upside down trapped in the cabin . . . we figured we'd get the railroad iron we kept for ballast and weight the cabin down so's it wouldn't blow away. . . . We sat around the cabin all day Saturday. . . . we didn't think of it to get worse and we had already discussed how we were going to right the boat, and so we just sat there all day Saturday and let come what would.

Nearby but unbeknownst to Tipp and his friends, Gid Scherer was encamped twelve miles out from the city with the U.S. Engineering Department on the shores of West Galveston Bay. "We were warned that a storm was coming but like every body else did not pay any attention to it," he wrote later. "Next morning we awoke to find water comming [sic] in our tents but we ate breakfast with out the least bit of fear." As the water continued to rise, the men moved onboard the sloop *Fever Island*, and Scherer recounted their travails:

We, eleven in number, staid [sic] in the cabin all that day, looking for some break in the storm. Late that evening it got worse and the boat began to drag her anchor which compelled us to chop out our mast to keep from capsizing. We went this way and that way all night, expecting to go to pieces every minute. Every one of us was as sick as any mortal ever got to be could not open any of the windows for fresh air as the water was all over our decks and would have filled her in a short while.

Activities at the port continued routinely. At the east end of the island five vessels floated at anchor in the Bolivar Roads waiting to enter the city. Three of them, the *Taunton*, *Hilarious*, and *Mexican* were British steamships in quarantine prior to entering the port. The *City of Everett* was also moored in Bolivar Roads, and the U.S. Army Corps of Engineers dredge boat, the *General C. B. Comstock*, was tied up at the Corps coal dock, which was connected to the south jetty. Twelve other vessels were already berthed along the city's wharves, and their officers and crews closely monitored the changing weather conditions. The first mate of the *Comino*, a steamer berthed at Pier 14, noted the squally weather, falling barometer, and rising water. By midmorning he ordered extra mooring lines put out as a safety measure and called for an anchor to be dropped as well. Captain W. R. Page of the English steamship *Taunton*, which was anchored offshore, ordered the engine room to get steam up so that he could ease the strain on the anchor. Jess and Bill Simpson, crew of a large two-masted schooner, *Hard Times*, decided to leave Pier 19 and sail their vessel farther up the bay. They planned to anchor near the mouth of the San Jacinto River and ride out the storm from there, but by around 2:00 in the afternoon when they were ready to leave, bay waters were too rough for the voyage. The two men took the schooner just north of Pelican Island and set three anchors to secure the vessel. With Pelican Island and Galveston Island between them and the Gulf of Mexico, the two men thought they would be protected from the worst of the storm, and settled in to ride it out.

Throughout Galveston, residents slowly began to understand that this would be no ordinary summer gale or "overflow." As the afternoon wore on, families gathered, workers left their employers, and businessmen hurried home to see after their friends and relatives. Ephraim Moore, who took orders and made deliveries for a local grocer, went home for lunch that Saturday, intending to complete his rounds after his meal. When he arrived at his residence, located near 41st Street and Avenue P, water already lapped at the piers supporting his house. His frightened wife and family refused to let him leave again, so he unloaded the remaining orders into the enclosed, dry area under his raised house and waited for the weather to pass. The Littlejohn family, who lived nearby, convened in their living room to hear about the washing away of the Pagoda bathhouse. Elbridge Gerry Littlejohn, a schoolteacher and principal of the Broadway school, had been downtown that morning and returned to the family home on Avenue O between 37th and 38th

Streets with news of the bad weather. Besides the destruction of the bathhouse, streetcars could no longer run through most of the city, and water was within a block of the Littlejohn house. As the wind and rain worsened, they moved upstairs.

Shortly before noon, Louisa Rollfing sent her son, August Rollfing Jr., to retrieve his father. Rollfing was working downtown, painting an office building, and told his son he would be home for lunch. When he arrived a little after noon he was surprised to find that his wife had not prepared a meal. They argued, and August promised to secure a carriage so that Louisa and the children could leave.

Police Chief Ketchum had gone to work that morning as usual, but as the day wore on, he found himself understaffed. Many of his men requested and received permission to move their families to safety as the weather worsened. By midafternoon he dispatched two officers and a patrol wagon to evacuate a family from a home at 6th Street and Winnie. Stymied by high water, the two men requisitioned a boat from a man in the neighborhood in order to complete the rescue. That done, the officers returned to headquarters, where only the chief and Officer E. M. Johnson remained.

All over the island, people began to appreciate the full extent of the danger. James Monroe Fendley and his family, like the Littlejohns, moved upstairs. He recalled that

the water rose so high downstairs that I put the children on the large dining room table, thinking it might be better in case the house went down to be on the lower floor and on the side next to the wind. When danger seemed imminent, I demanded attention and gave definite directions as to what each must do in case we were cast out into the storm. At this point, May [his daughter] keeled over unconscious and remained so until the danger had passed and many hours afterward. I took her upstairs on my shoulder, the wind from the front door striking me full on the back . . . I placed her on the bed, and then thru the black darkness I brought the others up and put them in the same room.

As Ephraim Moore and his family watched the water rise, they began to take precautions. They moved the stored groceries up into the house and put chickens from their flooded coop in a second-floor bedroom. The family dog joined the chickens later in the afternoon. Moore became even more afraid for the safety of his wife and children. He and a neighbor moved both of their families to Unger's grocery using a copper lined bathtub to carry their human freight. Unger's was already crowded with people seeking shelter when Moore and his cargo arrived.

Louisa Rollfing piled her children and some belongings into a carriage that August had sent from Malloy's livery stable. The weather was far too bad for the carriage to reach her first objective—August's mother's house. "It was a terrible trip," she recalled, "we could only go slowly for the electric wires were down everywhere, which made it so dangerous." Instead, she had the driver take the family to her sister- and brother-in-law's home at 36th Street and Broadway. She gave the driver one dollar for his careful transport and then recounted conditions on the eastern end of the island to her hosts.

When Isaac Cline went to his own home on Saturday afternoon, his route was treacherous. "Hurricane winds were driving timbers and slates through the air every where around me, splitting the paling and weather boarding of houses into splinters, and roofs of buildings were flying through the air." Being outside was beginning to carry hazards beyond the wind and waves themselves. Gusts over one hundred miles per hour turned wreckage into lethal weapons. Bricks flew through the air along with odd pieces of wood and masonry, uprooted shrubs, and tree limbs. Roof slates were especially dangerous. Like many nineteenth-century cities, Galveston had been plagued by fires, much of the damage a result of wooden building materials that became tinder for the blaze. After the worst conflagration in 1885, new regulations required slate roofs on buildings. Now the tiles became missiles in the gale, threatening to decapitate terrified islanders seeking safety.

Moving through waist-high water and dodging flying debris,

Cline arrived home to find fifty people besides his own brood gathered. His house was a relatively new structure, designed to withstand hurricane-force winds, and the recent builders sought cover there with their families. After dispatching his message over the Houston telephone line, Joseph Cline departed for Isaac's house as well, leaving the bureau office in the care of John Blagden. He went by way of the beach, still trying to warn people of the crisis. When they could not hear his voice over the howling wind, he gestured frantically toward downtown, hoping by gesticulation to urge them to higher ground and sturdier buildings. He brought bad news to the Clines; the barometer had continued to fall and was now below twenty-nine inches. By 3:00 P.M. water was three feet above the wharf; the few ships berthed there were being lashed by wreckage slammed into their hulls by winds and waves. About the same time Joseph Cline left the bureau office, Fred Langben and his brother left their desks at Jens Moller and Company, steamship agents. They tried to get home the usual way, south on 23rd Street to Sealy Avenue. Their trek was harrowing; tin roofs peeled back from buildings; telephone poles crashed onto streets and walkways; the power plant's brick smokestack swayed in the wind and fell. A block east on Sealy, the horse pulling their cart was blown off its feet and the brothers sprang out to help the animal regain its footing. Understandably nervous, the horse refused to pull the cart, so the Langbens led the beast back toward downtown and stabled him at a livery. At one point, Fred stepped off a curb and was immediately neck-high in water. The brothers took refuge in the telephone building, grateful to be indoors and safe, at least for the moment.

Earlier in the afternoon, Walter Grover and John Adriance had struggled to walk the streets, anxious to see the storm's fury for themselves. Adriance rapidly tired of the effort and returned home, and Grover fought to reach his residence as well. Like the Langbens, he tried to walk eastward down Sealy Avenue, keeping to the northern side of the street, his back to the worst of the wind. Grover finally reached home—the 1500 block of Avenue G

FIGURE 1.3: Scenes of horror greeted survivors on Sunday morning. Piles of debris kept water from draining away, and storm victims lay amidst the rubble. This was the view at 20th Street and Avenue M ¹/₂ at dawn, September 9, 1900. (Courtesy Prints and Photographs Division, Library of Congress, Washington, D.C.)

(Winnie)—sometime before 6:00 P.M. The last part of the way he worked his way fence post by fence post, swimming when necessary. His family, sure of his death, was overjoyed to see him, but the house was taking a beating. Water rushed in through broken doors and windows, and the chimney had collapsed. But for now, the family was safe and together.

Many Galvestonians, once they determined to seek higher ground, headed to the island's more substantial buildings, often institutions of some sort. St. Mary's University was a haven for some, and refugees gathered in a clubhouse building on the grounds. Rising water forced them to move to the main building later in the afternoon, and they made their way to the second floor. A cow greeted them there, and years after the storm, refugee Sydney Love still wonders how it got there, and, of greater interest, how it got down.

At St. Mary's Infirmary, a brick hospital several blocks to the northeast of the university at 8th Street and Avenue D (Market), hordes of neighborhood residents streamed into the building. The infirmary was the strongest building in the area, but that was a dubious distinction at best. Located at the far eastern end of the island, it was only six blocks from the Gulf and three blocks from the bay, surrounded by small frame houses. Patients now shared their space with people seeking shelter from the storm. The corridors were filled with terrified residents clutching what they had carried with them from their battered homes. Eventually nearly five hundred people sought safety at the infirmary. When windows blew out of a building housing about fifty elderly female patients, medical student Zachary Scott began moving them into the larger infirmary structure a half-block away. By the time he moved the last one, water was shoulder-high.

Sister M. Elizabeth Ryan had visited the infirmary earlier that day. In town to do shopping for St. Mary's Orphan Asylum, she stopped briefly to talk with Mother Gabriel but left as the weather turned worse. The orphanage, on the far western edge of the city and almost on the beach, was in a desolate spot and would be diffi-

cult to reach in the rising water. At the site, ten Sisters of Charity of the Incarnate Word and their ninety-three charges tried to prepare for the worst. Water had surrounded the building since early that morning, and everyone gathered on the second floor. With lengths of clothesline, the nuns tied the orphans together and then to the cinctures of their habits. While they watched, the boys' wing of the building collapsed from the pressure of wind and waves; not long afterward, the roof over them failed, falling inward onto the crowd. Nuns and orphans were crushed; three of the older children, all boys, were thrown out of the wreckage when the roof caved in. They clung to an uprooted tree, tying themselves to it with ropes already among the branches. Having made use of the ropes themselves, the three boys each wondered if others had tried to survive in this way. Even though the tree was swept into the Gulf of Mexico and then back onshore—eventually becoming entangled with the masts of a wrecked schooner, the *John S. Ames*— the boys survived.

As the water rose throughout the afternoon, Daisy Thorne, her family, and all of the others who came to Lucas Terrace for safety moved toward the stairs. Everyone, including the Thornes's five cats, moved to the second floor. As one of her last acts before retreating upstairs, Thorne's mother opened the downstairs doors to the water, hoping to lessen the pressure on the building.

Across town, George W. Boschke took a similar tack. When it became apparent that he, his family, and his guests would have to remain in the house, they opened all the doors and windows to "let the water anchor the house." Taking their evening meal from the dinner table, the family sat on the staircase, moving toward the second floor as the water rose inside the house.

Like many others, Louisa Rollfing and nine other people spent the storm barricaded in the house. As conditions worsened, they, too, moved up the stairs as water rose. "We soon heard the blinds and windows break in the rooms upstairs," she wrote later, and

[it] sounded as if the rooms were filled with a thousand little devils,

shrieking and whistling. In the rooms downstairs the furniture, even the piano, slid from one side of the rooms to the other and then back again. The water was up over the doors . . . over seven feet and if it kept rising more we would not be able to escape. We all prayed! . . . All at once something cracked. The kitchen broke loose from the house and left a big opening. It did not make much difference, as the house was full of water anyway. Soon after, the house was lifted off the brick pillars on two sides and now was hanging slanting.

Chief Ketchum realized that it was going to be a long night. Earlier, he had taken delivery of boots, a flannel shirt, and heavy pants packed and sent by his wife after a telephone call. His son, Henry, stayed at the station for a while, captivated by the increased activity, until his father sent him home. Like others that night, Henry dodged flying slate and debris and negotiated high water as he made his way home to the house on 31st Street. Sometime in the mid- to late afternoon bay waters and the Gulf of Mexico met and mingled across the island. Fully submerged, Galveston—and all that rested upon it—confronted a storm of unimagined ferocity.

The Tremont Hotel was packed. At the height of the storm watchers estimated that over one thousand people sought protection there. When Gulf waters began seeping into the lobby under the doors, guests headed for the stairs to the mezzanine. Like the Tremont, the Union Passenger Station became a refuge for many that night. Downtown businessmen unable to return home, travelers marooned by high water and canceled schedules, and workers who feared for the safety of their lodgings huddled together as the winds howled.

The storm battered ships in port unmercifully. On the *Comino*, the first mate recorded a barometer reading of 28.3 inches; wreckage from buildings pounded the vessel. In the midst of the terror, a board six inches wide and four feet long pierced the ship's plating, but the mooring lines held. Other ships in port were less fortunate. The *Roma*, berthed at Pier 15, put out anchors and every available line to no avail. Once the lines and anchors gave, the ship was

swept up the channel and into the freighter *Kendal Castle*. From there, *Roma* plowed through three railroad bridges and came to rest between the last railroad bridge and the wagon bridge that connected Galveston to the mainland. The *Kendal Castle* and three other vessels—*Guyller*, *Alamo*, and *Red Cross*—were driven away from the piers and run aground at various locations across the channel. The U.S. Army Corps of Engineers dredge, *General C. B. Comstock*, was blown from its berth at the coal dock to Pelican Spit. Only the *Comino* and *Norna* managed to stay at their berths.

Out in Bolivar Roads on the *Taunton*, the anchors—so carefully set by the captain as the hurricane approached—lost their hold, and the ship began to drift. With anchor chains snapped, the ship careened around the jetties propelled by wind and waves and was eventually thrown across Pelican Island and into shallower bay waters, and finally grounded near Cedar Point, almost thirty miles from where she had anchored.

Late Saturday night, on the far west end, P. G. Tipp and his fishing companions decided to brave the elements in an attempt to reach the city. Waiting all day in the overturned cabin of their boat, Will Jay and Christ Meyer began worrying about their families and sent Tipp out to survey the conditions. Years later he recalled that effort. "I crawled out the hole and as I started to go around the stern of the boat, the wind picked me up and threw me down like a tall weed. By laying in the water spread-eagled and crawling, I made it back to the boat." Unimpressed by his report, Jay and Meyer resolved to leave anyway. As Tipp recalled, the men

joined hands as we rounded the boat. The wind was fierce and the rain so bad you couldn't see or hear, and water was covering everything. It was black as nightmares and we didn't get too far when Will Jay was blown into the water. We broke hands and everyone scrambled for themselves. I seen Will Jay go under, with a funny look on his face and not saying a word. Christ and me landed in about ten feet of water and Christ yelled, "I can't even swim a lick." I ducked under the water and pulled off my clothes and shoes. Then from somewhere, Christ grabbed my leg and was pulling me wildly all over the place. I started swimming and Christ let go, and I swam with the wind, I didn't know where.

When the storm reached its peak between 6:00 and 8:00 P.M. that night, islanders knew that their circumstances were dire. Relentless pounding waves, wind gusts of extraordinary strength, and rising waters from the bay worked together to beat and batter the island's structures. Houses collapsed; they floated off their foundations; or they were crushed by masses of debris pushed by the wind and water. Shortly after 6:00 P.M. several people, including Isaac Cline, took note of a rapid rise in the water. Almost instantly, the water in the Clines's first floor rose four feet. Others remarked later upon a "giant swell" that swept down upon the island.

What they saw was the hurricane's "storm surge," a part of the storm most deadly for land masses—like Galveston—whose shorelines slope gradually into deeper water. As hurricanes build at sea, a column of churning water up to three hundred feet deep may develop beneath the storm's eye. Drawn upward as much as two feet by the low pressure at the center of the storm, this column of water may surge up to fifteen feet or more above sea level when it breaks across land. With a sloping shelf off of the coast, the column of water rises as it approaches, inundating the land in its path. In coastal waters with deep and abrupt shelving, the column of water dissipates against the sea floor or against underwater portions of the land mass; there may be a tidal rise of only a few feet. In hindsight, the exceptionally high tides that preceded the storm hinted at the size of the storm surge, but forecasters in 1900 knew far less about tropical cyclone mechanics. With passage of the storm surge, the worst had arrived. Houses that would have been safe under other circumstances were destroyed by breakers carrying tons of debris. Hundreds were thrown out of their homes or dragged beneath the waves as rooms collapsed around them.

At the Clines's, the water was now fifteen feet deep in the house.

The family and all of the others sheltered there were huddled in a room on the windward side; the brothers calculated that if the house were blown over, they would then be on the top wall and might be able to scramble out of the building. Wreckage pounded outside, and a trestle, still held together by its rails, drove in the side of the house. "The house creaked and was carried over into the surging waters and torn to pieces," Isaac Cline wrote later. Dragged underwater, Cline blacked out. When he regained consciousness, he found himself squeezed between two timbers. His youngest daughter was nearby, and in a lightning flash, he saw his other children and his brother clinging to wreckage. His wife had vanished. Years later he described the ordeal:

This struggle to live continued through one of the darkest of nights with only an occasional flash of lightning which revealed the terrible carnage about us. In order to avoid being killed by flying timbers, we placed the children in front of us, turned our backs to the winds and held planks, taken from the floating wreckage, to our backs to distribute and lighten the blows which the wind driven debris was showering upon us continually. . . . we could hear houses crashing under the impact of the wreckage hurled forward by the wind and storm tide, but this did not blot out the screams of the injured and dying.

The Clines floated in such a way until around 11:30 P.M., when the storm tide receded where they were and they could touch ground at 28th Street and Avenue P. People living close by took them in for the night.

At Lucas Terrace, the Thornes and their guests crowded into the second-floor parlor and listened to the roar around them. They were joined by several women and J. P. McCauley, a paralytic confined to his bed. The women, carrying McCauley, managed to cross over to the Thornes's by way of an ironing board stretched between the two residences. They entered on the third floor and went down to the Thornes's parlor. Waves smashed into the windows, and Mrs. Thorne began reading from the Bible. Over twenty

FIGURE 1.4: Many survivors recalled houses twisting and turning off their foundations. Galveston photographer H. H. Morris recorded this casualty of the hurricane. (Courtesy Rosenberg Library, Galveston, Texas.)

people packed themselves into Daisy Thorne's bedroom, a space that was in the rear of the building, away from the Gulf. A hallway in the apartment collapsed just as they crowded into the room, and the parlor crashed into the waves. Heavy timbers from construction at Fort Point were moving lethally down the shoreline, battering everything along the way. They pounded Lucas Terrace mercilessly until the greater portion of the building gave way.

The Littlejohns also moved upstairs, like many in flight from high water, and the family welcomed a German fisherman who had been fighting his way down the street to safety. As the wind blew the door open and shattered windows, Mrs. Littlejohn moved the family into the bathroom. "Mama stood on the edge of the bathtub and looked out of the window," Sarah Littlejohn wrote later,

my brother Harry sat on a little box where papa brushes his shoes. . . . The ceilings were leaking badly and the water felt so cold. We all were wet because the water was dripping down on us. The sounds we heard that night were just awful and the pipes sounded horrible.

Daniel Ransom, an African American, had built his own home near the beach. For health reasons he was a regular swimmer in the nearby Gulf, and he prepared to weather the storm at home. His house, however, like many others, was lifted off its foundation by the rising water, and he escaped the wreckage by diving into the swirling waves. For the next two-and-a-half hours, from 4:00 P.M. until 6:30 P.M., he rescued forty-five people from the roiling sea. He carried them to a sturdier brick building in the neighborhood, saving their lives in the process.

Race knew few boundaries at the height of the storm's fury. African American and white Galvestonians huddled together wherever they could gather safely—Ursuline Convent, Union Passenger Station, private homes—with little or no regard for southern racial codes. At the height of the storm, nearly one thousand people—black and white—filled Ursuline Convent. Four pregnant women gave birth that night; their babies were baptized immediately be-

cause few of those taking shelter there expected to survive.

At the Boschke home, neighbors and refugees filled the space. In addition to white friends and relatives of the family, black neighbors sought safety in the well-built home. The two groups concentrated in different areas—whites in one second-floor room, blacks in the hallway outside and a room nearby. As the wind and rain beat against the windows and walls, blacks began singing hymns to combat their fear. Mrs. Vidor, George Boschke, and others joined in. At G. W. Cleveland's home, located on the corner of 27th Street and Avenue Q, about fifty people—black and white—crammed into two upstairs rooms, "crowded together like sardines in a box." Sometime after 7 P.M., the house rolled over in the rush of water. Only five individuals survived: two white men, one white teenager, and two black children.

Across the channel, the stranded railroad passengers who sought refuge with the Bolivar lighthouse keeper moved from the house to the light itself. Claiborne and some of the men fought the wind to stretch ropes between the two structures, about fifty feet. Holding tightly to the line, the Claibornes and the stranded passengers moved from the house to the light. Once inside, the frightened people crept up the winding inside stairs of the light as the water rose ever higher. When the equipment that turned the light failed, H. C. Claiborne began to operate it manually. His wife helped, remarking, "I don't know who'll see it, but I'll help you turn it." Through the night, the lighthouse swayed.

The light at Fort Point was extinguished around 8:00 P.M. when one of the thick panes of glass surrounding the light was blown out by the force of the wind. Cut and bleeding, Charles Anderson returned to his house, where his wife dressed the wounds. The two sat and listened as railroad ties and rails, set loose by the storm, beat against the lighthouse supports.

Normal shift change at the police station was at 7 P.M., but this was no normal Saturday night. Chief Ketchum and three officers—and four hundred residents who sought refuge at City Hall—huddled together as the storm raged.

Sometime between 8 and 9 P.M. the water reached its highest

FIGURE 1.5: Over four hundred people sought refuge at City Hall during the hurricane. Police Chief Edwin Ketchum and two officers also spent the night there. This Nicholas Clayton designed building was severely damaged, but all of its refugees survived. (Courtesy Rosenberg Library, Galveston, Texas.)

level. Later, investigators calculated that it reached a depth of 15.7 feet at Henry Schutte's grocery store on the eastern end of the island, and 15.6 feet at St. Mary's Infirmary. Downtown, the water reached 10.5 feet at Union Station. Measurements were sometimes confusing. Besides being pushed and pulled by the wind, water was often held back by mounds of debris or kept from receding for the same reason.

Between 10:00 and 11:00 P.M. the worst passed, and water levels began to fall. Areas near the beach and the center of the island drained more slowly than the northern sections. Not only did winds continue to blow water onshore, but also the dam of debris created by the storm restricted the rapid recession of floodwaters. Louisa Rollfing remembered the water receding "about 12 o'clock." Slowly, gradually, people crept downstairs, crawled from under debris, or ventured outdoors. Sarah Littlejohn remembered the sight. "The water was about up to my knees and the mud and slime was plentiful. We went into the dining room and when we were in there mama said she saw something white through the window and we looked and saw it was a white cottage that had drifted there on the side of our house that night. Papa fixed the dining-room table so we could sleep on it then we children got up on it to go to sleep."

From the tiny rear bedroom at Lucas Terrace, Daisy Thorne saw the water receding. Of the sixty-four rooms in the building, only this one remained. It perched on the debris of the one below, an incongruous punctuation mark atop the rubble. Slowly, Thorne and those with her maneuvered through a window and outside. They still feared the structure's collapse and, with the storm's abatement, decided to wait for dawn amid the wreckage under the clearing sky.

Around 10 P.M., I. H. Kempner tied a rope around himself, handed the other end to a friend, and set out to find his coachman. Earlier, Kempner had sent the man to the stables, about forty feet behind the main house, to release the horses. Not finding the man or the horses (all were later found safe on a neighbor's porch),

FIGURE 1.6: Galveston Island was home to several U.S. Army installations. The rear emplacement of this battery at Fort San Jacinto was heavily damaged. ("Rear of Emplacement," Folder 062, Fort San Jacinto Dredges and Batteries 1902–1906, RG 077, National Archives Southwest Region, Fort Worth, Texas.)

Kempner struggled back to the house but noticed that the water seemed about a foot lower than before.

In the early hours of Sunday morning, the Claiborne family and their guests emerged from the Bolivar lighthouse and carefully, delicately explored their surroundings. Under a bright moon and clearing skies, they returned to the Claibornes's home and stayed until dawn. August Rollfing joined his family around 4 A.M. He had waited downtown that afternoon to pay his workers after sending the carriage for Louisa and the children. When none of the laborers came for their pay, he left for his mother's house, thinking Louisa and the children were there. Overcome by weather conditions, he spent the night moving from one structure to another as they were blown or swept away.

Mrs. George Boschke and her guests held a prayer meeting first thing Sunday morning, before confronting what awaited them in the wake of the hurricane. The two officers who had remained with Chief Ketchum left briefly to find their families; they returned later, after they had discovered that all of their relatives had been killed.

Gid Scherer and his unit spent the storm at sea.

When day broke, we were the most distressed looking crowd you ever saw. Could not see any land and could not tell where we were. Soon the sky cleared a little and we saw St. Louis pass [sic], the extreme west end of the Island. We were about twelve miles out in the Gulf, without a mast, our rudder gone, and boat in a sinking condition. No fresh water to drink and could not drink the salt. We made a small rail out of one of our tent poles and put an awning up for a sail. Made a rudder out of a plank . . .

The intrepid engineers managed to maneuver behind the west side of the island, secured water from "an English steamer" (perhaps the *Kendal Castle*), and arrived back in the city late Sunday evening.

P. G. Tipp, separated from his friends, spent most of the night clutching a four- by four-foot timber and managed to grab an even larger piece as he drifted. Tipp watched a cotton barge pass, heard cows bellowing, and finally lunged at a bundle of fence pickets. As daylight arrived he saw land in the distance and realized, gratefully, that he was being carried toward it. "After a while it got shallow," he wrote, "like up to my shoulders, so I left my driftwood go and waded for shore." Having earlier taken off his clothes and shoes, he picked up bits and pieces of clothing as he worked his way to a house on the shore. In it, he found four Italians, one seriously injured, none of whom could speak English. He managed to convey that he would go for help and began hiking to another house farther down the way.

Tipp was welcomed at the next house, given food and water, and directed toward the road to Alta Loma, a small town on the mainland. Upon arriving in Alta Loma, Tipp decided to return to Galveston because "everything was such a mess everywhere. Altaloma [sic] was washed nearly away, and everywhere there was mud and deserted prairie and piles of drift and snakes everywhere." Tipp stopped at Virginia Point and agreed to help a Captain Thornton sail a boatload of people to Galveston in exchange for free passage.

After about thirty minutes the breeze died out and we just drifted with the tide. We kept running into so many dead bodies that I had to go forward with a pike and shove the dead out of the way. There was never such a sight. Men, women, children, babies, all floating along with the tide. Hundreds of bodies going bump-bump, hitting the boat. I was sort of in a daze picking them out of the way. It was the most horrible thing I have ever seen.

Tipp and Captain Thornton finally reached Galveston and managed to tie up at 19th Street and Avenue B (Mechanic).

There had never been a worse disaster in North American history. The death toll, only approximate until much later, would eventually reach six thousand, the largest number of disaster fatalities ever recorded in American history. In a fifteen-hour period

FIGURE 1.7: St. Augustine Episcopal Church, after the storm. African American churches were decimated by the hurricane. Along with the buildings, years of records and historical information were also destroyed. (Courtesy Rosenberg Library, Galveston, Texas.)

FIGURE 1.8: St. Patrick's Catholic Church was one of the largest Catholic churches in the area, but that was a meager defense against the hurricane. Because of their design—large open interiors with peripheral walls— churches were especially vulnerable to the forces of wind and waves. (Courtesy Rosenberg Library, Galveston, Texas.)

FIGURE 1.9: By Sunday morning, the pleasant and comfortable business and residential landscape of Galveston had been replaced by a bewildering amalgamation of wreckage; building pieces, personal belongings, carts, wagons, trees, and human and animal corpses were stacked and scattered across vast portions of the island. (Courtesy Rosenberg Library, Galveston, Texas.)

FIGURE 1.10: Slowly, islanders began to work through the devastation. Some residents, mostly women and children, left the city. Workers collected the few remaining horses and wagons and started sorting through the wreckage. This area—Sealy Avenue around 12th Street—marked one edge of the debris line. Past these buildings, toward the beach, the island had been swept clean. (Courtesy Rosenberg Library, Galveston, Texas.)

FIGURE 1.11: Walking on the beach. In the far distance, the ruins of Sacred Heart Catholic Church rise above the wreckage. During the first week after the storm, workers combed the debris for bodies and began the slow process of clearing the detritus. (Courtesy Rosenberg Library, Galveston, Texas.)

FIGURE 1.12: Few parts of the island were exempt from destruction. This victim was found at 21st Street and Avenue O, in the eastern part of the city. (Courtesy Prints and Photographs Division, Library of Congress, Washington, D.C.)

FIGURE 1.13: Work crews and individuals searched for friends and family members among the bodies. At first, corpses were moved to makeshift morgues; valuables were taken to aid in identification. This victim was found on 23rd Street and Avenue P ½. Over twenty thousand people searched for loved ones. (Courtesy Prints and Photographs Division, Library of Congress, Washington, D.C.)

TABLE I. SAFFIR-SIMPSON SCALE OF HURRICANE INTENSITY

Category	Wind	Barometric Pressure	Storm Surge	Potential Damage
1	74 to 95 m.p.h.	More than 28.91 inches	4 to 5 feet	MINIMAL: Damage to trees, shrubbery, unanchored mobile homes.
2	96 to 110	28.50 to 28.91	6 to 8	MODERATE: Some trees blown down; major damage to exposed mobile homes; some damage to roofs.
3	111 to 130	27.91 to 28.47	9 to 12	EXTENSIVE: Trees stripped of foliage; large trees blown down; mobile homes destroyed; some structural damage to small buildings.
4	131 to 155	27.17 to 27.88	13 to 18	EXTREME: All signs blown down; extensive damage to windows, doors, and roofs; flooding inland as far as six miles; major damage to lower floors of structures near shore.
5	Greater than 155	Less than 27.17	Greater than 18	CATASTROPHIC: Severe damage to windows, doors, and roofs; small buildings overturned and blown away; major damage to structures less than 15 feet above sea level within 500 yards of shore.

Galveston had gone from the commercial emporium of the state to the nation's most tragic and demoralized city. The storm's power denuded segments of the island that had once been densely settled with homes, barns, trees, gardens, and people. Young Sarah Littlejohn reported the view from her home.

We looked out of the window and of all the beautiful homes that were between our house and the beach not one was left. It is just a clean sweep; nothing but desolation. I can hardly realize what has happened but when I look at the Gulf I knew we could not see it from our house before this storm and it seems so strange.

Beginning in 1971, hurricanes have been classified based upon a scale developed by Herbert Safir, an engineer, and Robert Simpson, former director of the National Hurricane Center. The Safir Simpson scale sorts storms based upon wind speed, barometric pressure, and storm surge. A category 1 storm, for example, has winds that range in speed from 74 to 95 miles per hour, a barometric pressure above 28.91 inches, and a storm surge of four to five feet. Category 5 storms are the worst, with winds above 155 miles per hour, pressure below 27.17, and a storm surge over eighteen feet. According to this system, the storm that hit Galveston was probably a category 4. Wind gauges gave way long before the height of the storm, and the storm surge was later calculated to have been approximately fifteen feet (see Table 1).

The hurricane cut a swath of death and destruction to the south side of the city, along the coast, and to the east. In a fifteen-hundred-acre crescent from the far east end of the island at 8th Street

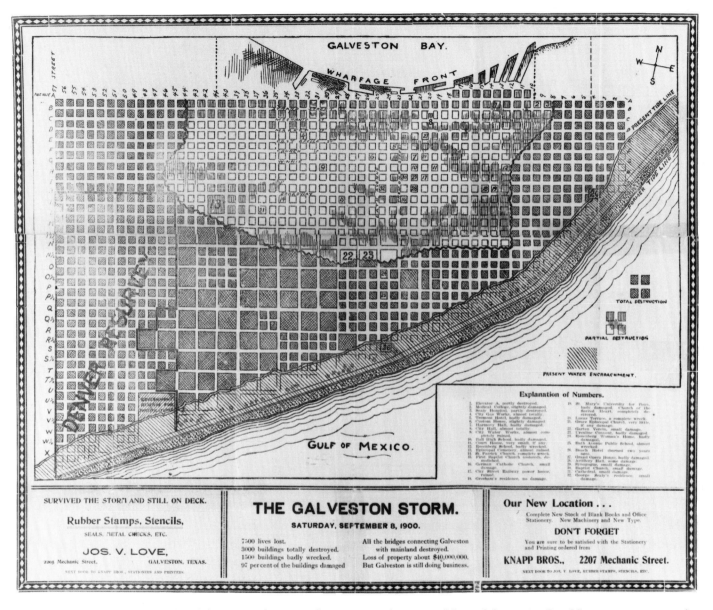

FIGURE 1.14: Local businesses produced this map to document the hurricane's destruction. Different types of shading identified "total destruction," "partial destruction," and "present water encroachment." (Courtesy Rosenberg Library, Galveston, Texas.)

diagonally across Broadway to the shore and away to the west end of the island beyond 45th Street, it appeared as if a giant scythe had cleared the land.

Whole neighborhoods were swept away, leaving behind only a bare marshy stretch of soil from the Gulf to Avenue P. Structures closest to the beach were the first to succumb to the waves and wind—a lethal combination that rocked the clapboard houses off their foundations. As the structures collapsed, they broke apart, becoming floating weapons, torpedoes that struck other struggling buildings, driving them from their piers and pilings. A battering ram made of former dwellings and powered by fifteen- to thirty-foot waves and hurricane-force winds beat against everything in its path for hours until all came to rest in a thirty-foot high, three-mile-long mountain of refuse and debris just south of Broadway.

In this tangled and tortured mound of detritus rested the remains of hapless victims, now sodden corpses, dead animals, machinery, fences, barns, homes, and furnishings. Aside from the human fatalities, property losses were staggering. Approximately four thousand—nearly two thirds—of the city's structures were demolished; Galvestonians lost between $17 and $30 million worth of property. All four bridges—railroad and wagon—to the mainland were destroyed, plus telegraph, telephone, and electrical lines. The only access to the island was by boat, the only light from candle and kerosene lantern. Trains, streetcars, and the island's water pumping station were immobilized. In the deathly stillness of Sunday morning, in the almost apologetic brilliance of sunshine and blue sky, the only sounds came from the pealing of bells of the Ursuline Convent and from urgent cries of injury and anguish.

CHAPTER TWO

"You brave people of Galveston"

From Wreckage to Recovery

The sea, with its fury spent, had sullenly retired. The strongest buildings, half standing roofless and tottering, told what once had been the make-up of a thriving city.

CLARA BARTON

THE WORLD NEEDED to know about the disaster! At about 10 A.M. on Sunday, September 9, a group of civic leaders considered how to get word off the island. But who would cross a still-boisterous bay now littered with debris and corpses? What boat had survived the hurricane? Somehow the *Pherabe*, a twenty-foot-long steam launch, had managed to keep her moorings. She left Sunday morning at 11 A.M. with a messenger force of six men—two journalists, two brokers, an engineer, and a contractor. The frail vessel maneuvered the roily sea and its flotsam to make the ten-mile trip across the bay.

Finally arriving at Texas City, the crew waded ashore and made their way to the town of La Marque, where they found a rail hand-car. So important was the mission that each man vowed that if he had to end his journey due to exhaustion, the others would leave him and go on. In the midst of pumping the fifteen miles north-ward to League City, they met an oncoming train, which at first refused to turn around. The five men climbed aboard and retraced their path south until the track gave out, whereupon the conductor headed back to Houston. The emissaries cabled Texas governor Joseph D. Sayers and President William McKinley at 3 A.M. Monday, September 10. The telegraphed message began, "I have been de-putized by the mayor and Citizen's Committee of Galveston to in-form you that the city of Galveston is in ruins . . . ." The president wired Governor Sayers his sympathy and promised "whatever help it is possible to give shall be promptly extended. Have directed the secretary of war to supply rations and tents upon your request."

Houston, already anticipating a relief operation for Galveston, responded immediately and admirably. A party of 250 volunteers left Houston at 4 A.M. Monday with a railcar load of provisions. A steamer bringing two more carloads of supplies and one hundred thousand gallons of fresh water departed for the island shortly thereafter. A special train took the rescuers, equipped with passes from Houston relief mayor L. H. Brashear, to within five miles of the bay, where they walked and carted the goods to the shore. A small party rowed across the bay and arrived in Galveston at 1 P.M.—the first group to bring word of relief and manpower waiting to enter the stricken city. Slowly and in shifts rescuers came, some to aid in recovery, others to search for loved ones. Passage over the bay, as P. G. Tipp found out, eerily presaged conditions on the island. One father looked into the face of "every light haired woman with a child in her arms" that floated by thinking it might be his daughter. A. M. Shannon rode the relief train from Houston and worried: "This was the time that tried men's souls . . . Until I reached Galveston, I did not know whether my mother, sister, and three brothers had weathered the storm or not, but on reaching home found they had." Gordon Gaither wrote of steeling himself for the journey, recalling that he saw "one lone flickering light . . . what a gruesome sight met our gaze and it was made more appalling because it was night."

While the six messengers made their way north, Mayor Walter C. Jones called a meeting of citizens at 2 P.M. on Sunday at the Chamber of Commerce rooms in the Tremont Hotel "for the purpose of organizing to relieve the suffering and to bury the dead." Their first act was to create the Central Relief Committee for Galveston Storm Sufferers (CRC) with Mayor Jones as chairman and eight members—Bertrand Adoue, John Sealy, Isaac H. ("Ike") Kempner, Jens Moller, William A. McVitie, Ben Levy, Morris Lasker, and Daniel Ripley. Subcommittees were then formed to handle the emergency. Public safety was a critical issue, and J. H. Hawley agreed to handle property protection and public safety in cooperation with Chief of Police Edwin Ketchum, who warned that looters were stealing food and provisions. The only way to control this was to declare martial law and ask for a volunteer militia to ward off looting, close saloons, and requisition (and pay for) foodstuffs for distribution. The injured were desperate for medical care. Daniel Ripley chaired the hospital committee, which was made up of two medical doctors and three clergymen, among them Father James M. Kirwin and Rabbi Henry Cohen, the latter of whom was the first person to reach the hospitals with food. Ben Levy chaired a burial committee of six and requested that inquests on the dead be suspended to prevent delay in burying the (grossly underestimated) four hundred to six hundred bodies that they anticipated recovering. Mayor Jones called a special meeting of the city council to pass a measure suspending inquests. One of the gravest matters was an absence of fresh water for human and animal consumption and for fighting fires. The island's water supply came from artesian wells on the mainland. A thirty-six-inch main under the bay carried the water to the city pumping station, from which it was distributed to households and businesses. The main had weathered the storm, but the pumping station stood in shambles. Over a hundred men worked to restore the water supply system.

Morris Lasker and five others, mainly journalists, comprised the correspondence committee, which was charged with publicizing the city's needs. John Sealy took on the task of treasurer and headed a finance committee of six with Adoue, Kempner, Moller, and W. L. Moody Jr. assisting. Moller proposed a plan to get money from the federal government, while Galveston's printers, Clarke and Courts Co., said they would advance all the money immediately necessary. Later D. B. Henderson was designated to head a committee overseeing transportation of people and goods to and from the island. McVitie presided over the important relief committee (a subcommittee of the CRC), which had twenty-five members. That evening and the next morning they met and organized assistance efforts by wards, electing a chairman for each. Tasks assigned to ward chairmen included finding a central store or house from which to distribute relief items, ordering goods from wholesale grocers, having assistants available to distribute goods from 7 A.M. to 6 P.M. each day, beginning debris cleanup, and meeting daily for conference at 9 A.M. Civic leaders who served as

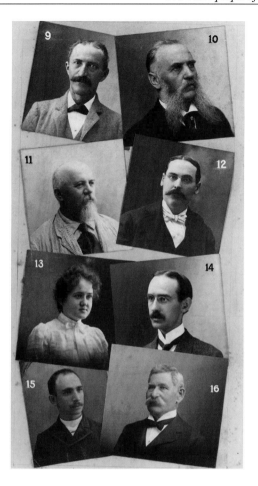

FIGURE 2.1: Members of the Central Relief Committee. 1. Clara Barton, president of the American National Red Cross. 2. Walter C. Jones, mayor and chairman of the CRC. 3. William A. McVitie, ship agent and chairman of the relief committee. 4. John Sealy, banker and chairman of the finance committee. 5. R. V. Davidson, state senator and CRC secretary. 6. Isaac H. Kempner, financier and member of the finance committee. 7. Noah Allen, city recorder and chairman of the Relief Labor Bureau. 8. Daniel Ripley, ship agent, chairman of the hospital committee and chairman of the transportation committee. Insert—Stephen E. Barton, nephew of Clara Barton and general manager of Red Cross operations in Galveston. (Courtesy Rosenberg Library, Galveston, Texas.)

FIGURE 2.2: Members of the Central Relief Committee. 9. Ben Levy, alderman and chairman of the burial committee. 10. Jens Moller, ship agent, member of the finance committee and chairman of the labor committee. 11. Bertrand Adoue, banker, member of the finance committee and chairman of the building committee. 12. William V. McConn, labor *Journal* editor and member of the building committee. 13. Miss Williams, official stenographer. 14. Dr. George A. Soper, honorary member and sanitation expert. 15. Reverend Henry Cohen, rabbi of Temple B'nai Israel and member of the hospital committee. 16. Morris Lasker, businessman, chairman of the correspondence committee and member of the building committee. (Courtesy Rosenberg Library, Galveston, Texas.)

needed were Noah Allen, William V. McConn, and R. V. Davidson, with a Miss Williams as stenographer. When Clara Barton arrived, she was invited to become a member, as was Dr. George A. Soper, who would serve in an honorary capacity as advisor for sanitation. No African American served on the central committee, a mistake that brought tragic consequences.

Soon the city discovered that the death toll and damage far exceeded early estimates. Headlines in the Galveston *Daily News* blared that the loss of life approached five thousand souls and property damage reached between $15 and $20 million. Both estimates missed the mark. The job of removing the bodies that littered the streets was so ghastly that strong men recoiled from the spectacle. Recruits had to be rounded up. Some covered their noses with camphor-soaked handkerchiefs and plowed ahead. Father James M. Kirwin, rector of St. Mary's Cathedral and a temperance man, concluded that "men could not handle those bodies without stimulants." In a mission of mercy he gave them whisky. Workmen loaded the bodies onto carts and wagons, then directed their cargo toward the city's undertakers and a crude temporary morgue on the north side of the Strand between 21st and 22nd Streets. Hundreds of corpses waited for identification—a futile effort, since loved ones searching for lost relatives had no place to bury them anyway.

As the death count mounted it became clear that mass burial was out of the question because the earth was too soaked. In the packed death houses bodies decayed and fell apart in the summer heat. Survivors believed that without quick action, the living would be among the dead; burial at sea seemed the only solution. On Monday evening, men loaded some seven hundred bodies onto three waiting barges. Deputized citizens forced fifty black men at bayonet point to board these barges and to assist with the grim task of body disposal. They transported the cargo eighteen miles into the Gulf of Mexico, waited all night, fastened iron weights to the corpses, and cast them overboard.

To everyone's horror, the remains washed ashore, some with two-hundred-pound weights. After hearing the grisly news, Ida Austin penned these sorrowful lines. "The sea as though it could never be satisfied with its gruesome work washed these bodies back upon the shore, the waves being the hearses that carried them in to be buried under the sand." Poetic eulogies could not hide the fact that according to the Galveston *Daily News* the dead were "decomposing rapidly and giving off a horrible stench. . . . On Tuesday morning the bodies had decomposed so greatly that it was absolutely impossible to handle them to send them to sea." At that point, despite conditions, some of the remains were hastily buried in the sand.

Corpses in the sand and on the streets constituted only the most visible problem for the city. P. G. Tipp found it difficult to walk: "There were so many dead, you would sink into the silt onto a body at every other step. . . . The vermin were out and you had to chase the rats off the dead most of the time." Thousands of animal carcasses lay putrefying along with human remains under mounds of debris.

In the 88-degree heat of September, survivors predicted an epidemic. The only response, the city's medical community intoned, was to remove the bodies from the debris and cremate them in great funeral pyres on the beaches.

Charnal mounds—incinerating up to twelve corpses at a time—burned into November, smoky and smelling of smoldering flesh and hair. "They gathered up all the dead bodies they could find," noted Daniel Ransom. "Then they piled them up, just like you cross-pile cord wood, and pour oil all over them and burn them. It sure was a awful sight, but I guess it was all they could do." Tipp, who at age eighteen headed up a team of eight "negroes," recalled that they dug "a bunch of huge pits, and after searching for bodies for identification and valuables, we built up a roaring fire in the pit and threw them in. We were working on 25th and O ½ streets and we burnt up over five hundred bodies. . . ." By November, wrote Tipp, he "had done so much burning, and so much work that I just gave out. I was sick for a long time. I can still smell the dead, and the burning bodies, like burnt sugar."

From across the bay, Fannie B. Ward of the Red Cross commented on the burning pyres.

FIGURE 2.3: Workmen loaded bodies onto carts at 22nd Street and the Wharf. Seventy-three wagon loads of victims were carried to the morgue and the barges for disposal. Photograph by W. A. Green. (Courtesy Prints and Photographs Division, Library of Congress, Washington, D.C.)

FIGURE 2.4: Makeshift morgues like this one were intended to help the survivors identify their family members, but often there were no survivors in a family and no place to bury them. (Courtesy Rosenberg Library, Galveston, Texas.)

FIGURE 2.5: Barges were stacked with seven hundred bodies ready for burial at sea. The crew traveled eighteen miles offshore with their grim cargo on Monday evening, September 10, and waited until dawn to throw the corpses overboard. The remains washed ashore even though weighted down, some with two-hundred-pound iron fastenings. (Courtesy Rosenberg Library, Galveston, Texas.)

FIGURE 2.6: Workmen struggled to remove this corpse from under sand and twenty feet of debris. (Courtesy Prints and Photographs Division, Library of Congress, Washington, D.C.)

FIGURE 2.7: The beaches were strewn with the dead. This corpse, swollen from the heat, is readied for cremation. (Courtesy Rosenberg Library, Galveston, Texas.)

FIGURE 2.8: Crews of men transported bodies to the cremation pyres.
(Courtesy Prints and Photographs Division, Library of Congress,
Washington, D.C.)

FIGURE 2.9: The tents in the background show that the homeless, who stayed in these temporary quarters, were within sight of the removal of the dead. This corpse is being carried away to be burned. (Courtesy Prints and Photographs Division, Library of Congress, Washington, D.C.)

FIGURE 2.10: These workmen are preparing to consign a storm victim to the flames. (Courtesy Prints and Photographs Division, Library of Congress, Washington, D.C.)

Over on Galveston island, a long line of flame, mounting to the heavens, marked the burning of ruined homes and corpses; while other fires, in all directions on the mainland, told of similar ghastly cremations. . . . Early in the morning a strange odor drew attention to a fresh funeral-pyre, only a few rods away. . . . That peculiar smell of burning flesh, so sickening at first, became horribly familiar within the next two months, when we lived in it and breathed it, ate it and drank it, day after day.

Workers uncovered about seventy bodies a day for the first month, but removing corpses from the tangled mounds of wreckage became increasingly difficult. Ward continued,

In the hot moist atmosphere of the tropics, decomposition had so far advanced that the corpses—which at first were decently carried in carts, or on stretchers, then shoveled upon boards or blankets—had finally to be scooped up with pitchforks, in the hands of negroes, kept at their awful task by the soldiers' bayonets. . . . The once beautiful driving beach was strewn with mounds and trenches, holding unrecognized and uncoffined victims.

Although repelled by the sight, Fannie Ward investigated one of the "primitive crematories" and found the tender adding "boards, water-soaked mattresses, rags from blankets and curtains, part of a piano and the framework of sewing-machines. . . ." But this was merely fuel for the fire's real purpose, burning for a month some sixty human bodies plus dogs, cats, hens, and cows. The day before, seven bodies had been consigned to the fire, but they were only "baked" because, as the custodian explained, it took a corpse several days to burn completely. He thought that about a dozen had recently been reduced to "just bones" at the bottom of the pile. Pathos mingled with his brusque description. That day a young woman, tall and slim, with long brown hair and wearing a blue silk skirt had been added to his pyre. He commented that "there was a rope tied around her waist, as if somebody had tried to save her." Fannie Ward picked up a lock of yellow hair, wept, and wondered, "what mother's hand had lately caressed it."

For many dazed islanders the only option was departure. Shocked, fearful of disease, plagued by shortages of housing and food, or stunned by the dreadful scene of devastation, thousands of survivors opted to leave the island as soon as transportation could be arranged. An exodus of nearly ten thousand people, mostly women and children, began in the days after the disaster.

The city's population, according to the 1900 census, stood at 37,789. Surveys conducted just after the storm indicated that the city lost 32 percent, or nearly twelve thousand, of its population. The actual death count for the city has never been calculated, but if six thousand lives were lost (the most widely used number), then another six thousand people left within the first month. Red Cross workers met the desolate survivors at Texas City and reported what they saw.

Each trip to the mainland, the boat came filled with refugees from the city of doom—the sick, the maimed, the sorrowing—many with fearful bodily injuries inflicted by the storm, and others with deeper wounds of grief—mothers whose babies had been torn from their arms, children whose parents were missing, fathers whose entire families were lost—a dazed and tearless throng, such as Dante might have met in his passage through Inferno.

Later passengers leaving the island were ferried in barges. Louisa Rollfing recalled that on her barge "a railing of boards was nailed all around and in this enclosure we all stood like cattle in a pen. It was packed with women and children." Once these people arrived in Houston, they were escorted to a hospitality and relief station, given food and lodging, and helped with transportation needs. The Gulf, Colorado, and Santa Fe Railway furnished free passage for the destitute to anywhere along their route in Texas.

For those who chose or who were forced to remain (men were not allowed to leave at first, only women and children), security became a primary issue. As soon as the Central Relief Committee

FIGURE 2.11: An exodus of nearly ten thousand people, mostly women and children, began days after the disaster. This boat waits to transport survivors to the mainland. (Courtesy Prints and Photographs Division, Library of Congress, Washington, D.C.)

held its first meetings, offers to aid in policing came from the white Screwmen's Benevolent Association, the city's most influential union. Members voted to give one thousand dollars to the CRC and volunteered to be at the disposal of the committee in policing, clearing streets, or any activity deemed appropriate by the leaders. The next day, September 11, the African American screwmen, known as the Cotton Jammers' Association, offered their services as well. The Central Relief Committee appointed the white screwmen to police and clear the island in the days before the Texas militia arrived, while it appointed black screwmen only to clearing the debris, a case of favoritism that reflected white fears of armed blacks.

The need for security was great; the police force numbered seventy, not enough manpower to protect the populace from looters. Mayor Jones closed the saloons and deputized temporary officers, some of them armed, but the city needed a military presence. To safeguard the wholesale warehouses and the makeshift commissaries, to ensure order in the city, and to protect the public, Mayor Jones on September 13 called in Texas militia men under the leadership of Brigadier General Thomas Scurry. Earlier, several individuals suspected of looting had been shot by local patrollers. To end the uncertainty and to secure the island, Scurry declared martial law on September 13, issued twenty-four general orders, and compelled guardsmen to help remove women and children and to establish tents for the homeless.

The relief committee of the CRC began its work immediately by dividing relief operations among the twelve city wards and establishing a "commissary," or relief station, that was supervised by an elected ward chairman and his appointed committee in each section. At first the only supplies available were from grocers and wholesale houses on the island. Goods were purchased by the CRC for immediate distribution so that hunger was kept at bay. For the first week stores were given out liberally to the survivors because needs were pressing, and laborers responsible for cleanup were not yet being paid. Ward chairmen organized a workforce with horses and drays to remove bodies and debris and warned that "Any able-bodied man who will not volunteer for this work must not be fed."

By September 15 a force of one to two thousand men—some of them from the white Screwmen's Benevolent Association and the black Cotton Jammers' Association—assembled to clear wreckage from streets and alleys, create passageways, retrieve bodies, and disinfect the city, often by spreading lime over fetid water and carcasses.

According to J. H. Parker, who served as foreman of the streets and alleys department, the men also dug drainage ditches so that standing water, some of it two feet deep and "foul and smelling bad," could run off into the Gulf. He reported that he appointed four men to "cut all wires that obstruct opened streets, also to plug all pipes where city water is running to waste." The provision that no man be fed unless he worked was based on the fact that in the beginning the CRC had no money with which to pay workers. Instead, laborers received rations from the commissaries until funds became available to pay them $1.50 to $2.00 a day after September 18. They were then expected to buy food and supplies; those who received rations thereafter—women, children, and elderly or disabled men—were considered truly dependent because there was no able-bodied worker in the household.

Every day at the Tremont Hotel, the ward chairmen met, exchanged information, and reported on their neighbors' needs. Food at first was not plentiful. As Henry Wolfram described it,

hunger soon asserted itself, the grown folks could pretty well stand it, but with the poor children it was quite different, cold, shivering and half naked they clamored for food, our stoves were ruined, the cupboards washed clean by the lashing waves of their contents . . . for a week or more, we were leaning our weight on Soda Crackers. . . .

At the end of the first week food began coming from the mainland, saving committee funds for the purchase of goods that would provide for residents' more long-term needs. Wolfram added, "it is a great and wonderful sight to behold the immense amount daily arriving; there is absolutely no danger of starvation." Among many donors, the Merchants' Association of New York "dispatched a gov-

FIGURE 2.12: By September 15 a force of one to two thousand men—some of them from the white Screwmen's Benevolent Association and the black Cotton Jammers' Association—assembled to clear wreckage from streets and alleys, create passageways, retrieve bodies, and disinfect the city. Here a biracial workforce of about twenty-five pauses for the photographer. (Courtesy Rosenberg Library, Galveston, Texas.)

ernment vessel to Galveston laden with food and necessaries. . . ."
J. H. Hawley wrote that by September 18 the whole world seemed
"to have arisen in sympathy and help is coming from Paris, Bremen,
Liverpool, London, Hamburg, as well as provisions, nurses, physi-
cians and other offerings are coming from every portion and part
of the country." Andrew Carnegie sent $20,000; Standard Oil,
$10,000; the New York Chamber of Commerce, $65,800. The king
of Italy, the president of France, and Kaiser Wilhelm of Germany
wired their condolences. Food was the first item required, but the
city would need supplies of clothing, shoes, cots, bedding, household furnishings, stoves, sewing machines, and substantial dwellings
for the eight to ten thousand homeless Galvestonians. Outside organizations—merchants' associations, the U.S. Army, the Salvation
Army, the Children's Aid Society, the Afro-American Press Association—began to send supplies. At this point, the Red Cross, with its
access to national generosity, entered Galveston.

Clara Barton, the seventy-eight-year-old president of the American National Red Cross, heard about the disaster on September 10
just after returning to Washington, D.C., from Chicago. Still fatigued from her journey and not feeling in the best of health,
Barton nonetheless prepared to answer the call. She sent word to
her long and trusted Texas friend, Austin politician Alexander W.
Terrell, and offered the services of the American National Red
Cross. Then, against the advice of her friends and the judgment of
the Red Cross Board of Control, she hurried to the island in the
company of three ladies and five gentlemen. The New York *World*
made her an offer she could not refuse: it would provide a palace-
car for transportation to Galveston, and the newspaper would give
all funds donated to it to the Red Cross, a sum that reached nearly
two thousand dollars.

Setting out on the 13th, the party traveled via Atlanta and New
Orleans to Houston, where they met delegations from the governor's committee for relief work and from the mayor, who offered
transportation to the island. The journey to Galveston took twenty-
four hours with a night's delay in Texas City, where the Red Cross
band was given tinned beef, bread, and coffee by the Salvation

FIGURE 2.13: Clara Barton, president of the American National Red Cross
Association, posed for this portrait August 23, 1904. (Courtesy Prints and
Photographs Division, Library of Congress, Washington, D.C.)

Army. Early Monday, September 17, a boat arrived bearing "fleeing women and children, dressed in whatever had been left them or given by the charitably inclined." Only those with passes from the mayor of Houston were allowed to make the journey by steamer across the bay. Red Cross workers finally arrived in Galveston on September 17, nine days after the hurricane. They met Mayor Jones at the wharf and were driven to the Tremont Hotel. Along the way they encountered a soldiers' camp, and the men cheered Clara Barton and the Red Cross. At the hotel they were met by more officers who welcomed them as Red Cross nurses. Although nursing had been among the initial duties of organization volunteers upon its founding in 1881, these employees of the Red Cross had come to administer relief. Not sure exactly what the Red Cross would be doing, city leaders soon learned that they were there to aid city relief workers and disaster victims.

After the initial meeting, Clara Barton, feeling ill from the "gripe," took to her bed in the Tremont Hotel, causing some in her party to suspect that she was too old and frail for this kind of work. In fact, it would be the last such on-site emergency relief work that she would personally attend. Plans to send the redoubtable Barton back to Washington were swept aside as she rallied to direct operations from a daybed in her hotel room. Incensed that others would presume to banish her, she labeled the attempt "a piece of nonsense which I both forbid and rebuked. I was quite well, in three or four days and have been able to conduct my part of the work without interruption." Her nephew, Stephen E. Barton, arrived on September 18 to bolster his ailing aunt and dispel the rumors of her imminent collapse. He also took on the tasks of general manager under her supervision. His first communication by telegraph stated: "Property destruction is simply apalling [sic]. Extent is not half realized."

As soon as possible Red Cross workers toured the disaster site. Stunned, Clara Barton wrote,

It was one of those monstrosities of nature which defied exaggeration and fiendishly laughed at all tame attempts of words to picture the scene it had prepared. The churches, the great business houses, the elegant residences of the cultured and opulent, the modest little homes of laborers of a city of nearly forty thousand people; the center of foreign shipping and railroad traffic lay in splinters and debris piled twenty feet above the surface, and the crushed bodies, dead and dying, of nearly ten thousand of its citizens lay under them.

Once the scene had been absorbed, Red Cross workers shook off their dismay and set about establishing headquarters. The organization was there to help in the emergency by entering into partnership with the local Central Relief Committee. It brought trained personnel best suited to raise needed funds nationally and to distribute relief goods promptly with the least amount of discord. The Red Cross strove not to take over existing arrangements for emergency relief but to work within them. They hoped to bolster local leadership and avoid criticism as a source of outside interference.

Based on countless experiences with flood victims, Red Cross workers had developed a systematic way of addressing disaster relief. They knew that the greatest problems stemmed from property losses and public health and sanitation. In the first stage of its mission—the period of emergency relief—Red Cross workers did their best to provide food, clothing, and household furnishings. Knowing that the organization could never entirely replace lost property, it considered the family to be "the unit of treatment," and rationed goods according to need rather than according to losses endured. Once families had been helped over the initial shock and had received enough to sustain them, the next stage—rehabilitation—began. According to Red Cross instructions, "rehabilitation plans and acts for ultimate welfare"; hence each family's particular needs were ascertained in order to reestablish a home and work for the future. The first stage of emergency relief lasted approximately two weeks, although as word of the disaster reached the nation, supplies and money continued to flow into the city as late as December and January.

By September 19, John Sealy had donated a four-story warehouse at 25th Street and the Strand for a Red Cross headquarters and warehouse. In response to a call for donations, letters came pouring in. The overworked staff, and even Barton herself with the help of her "stenographer and one or two lady friends," kept track of all donations, wrote thank-you letters, instructed donors what to send and where to send it, forwarded packages to relatives in the area, saw dignitaries, and calmed supplicants.

The value of having Clara Barton, president of the American National Red Cross, give her personal attention to Galveston cannot be underestimated. Although there were others in the organization who managed the detail work, her reputation and that of the Red Cross were what inspired the country to send money and supplies. Because of her long practice of rushing to the sites of disasters and wars in order to bring relief, she had won the trust of Americans of all races. She reported back to Red Cross headquarters in Washington, D.C., almost instantly that "the conditions in Galveston have not been exaggerated by the public press." She and her vice presidents wrote reports for public release, which the Red Cross sent to the Washington *Post* and the Associated Press, and editors responded warmly. "The people know in whom they have trusted and will trust you ever more." Her words verified that the tragedy was real and that relief gifts would be handled through the Red Cross, lest donors worry that a badly managed or corrupt city government misuse the donations. A woman from Rathbone, Ohio, wrote, "I have been wishing ever since I knew of the disaster in Galveston that I knew to whom to send money so that it would be sure of reaching some needy person and was very glad when I saw by the papers that you are there."

Barton continued to send reports: "Devastation is terrible. Millions of aid needed. . . . The need here is tenfold greater than has yet to be reported." These words, penned by one of America's most revered figures, had the desired effect, although hoped-for millions did not materialize. She was a catalyst for recovery, drawing money and supplies from loyal supporters and from strangers who knew no one in Galveston but recognized the name Clara Barton. She also had numerous friends and did not hesitate to ask for help. To the Woman's Relief Association of Algiers, Louisiana, she wired,

FIGURE 2.14: The headquarters for the American National Red Cross in Galveston was this four-story warehouse at 25th Street and the Strand. John Sealy donated the building and the volunteers quickly turned it into a distribution center for donated items, an orphanage, a kitchen, and a dormitory for Red Cross workers. (Courtesy Galveston County Historical Museum, Galveston, Texas.)

"Need immediately sheets, pillow cases and necessary bedding for one hundred cots for Orphans Home." She directed dispatchers in New York City to take all donations for the Red Cross straight away to the Mallory Line for shipment to Galveston. She sent appeals for money to the National Commander of the Grand Army of the Republic and to the Woman's Relief Corps. She even wrote President William McKinley.

Such a reputation made it possible for Galveston to be the beneficiary not only of unsolicited donors but also of exceedingly efficient Red Cross societies across the nation. These were among the most active and generous of donors. By September 19, the Associate Society of the Red Cross of Philadelphia had wired one thousand dollars. This large donation brought paeans of praise from Barton:

I am very deeply touched by the filial thought of the old Red Cross societies on this occasion. New Orleans stands like a rock—Dear old Dansville [New York], the first Red Cross society that ever formed, remembers only us and all comes with such words of loving appreciation that it makes the thought of the work of a hard life easy.

Red Cross auxiliaries in places like San Francisco (eleven boxes, two trunks); New Orleans; Frederick, Maryland ($571.85); and Reno, Nevada, responded with amazing alacrity to the emergency.

She was able to let the nation know what was needed and in what quantity. The first call went out for disinfectants, "to protect the living against the dead." The New York *World* responded by sending via barge fifty-seven barrels of carbolic acid and two thousand pounds of miscellaneous disinfectants, which the Red Cross turned over to the CRC. In September, too much heavy winter clothing had arrived, and she pleaded for cash donations to buy from local merchants (at sacrifice prices) articles that were needed. This system was thus able to "in that way minister to the wants of the suffering and encourage the merchants whose trade is stagnated by the overwhelming disaster." She and Stephen Barton declared in nearly every letter they wrote responding to questions that for the work of buying goods and medicines from local merchants and for the work of relief

nothing is so much needed as money forwarded or telegraphed to the National Red Cross at once. . . . The great relief must come in the form of many millions of dollars, . . . which must be poured in to partially reinstate those whose dwellings and contents have been absolutely annihilated to the number of many thousands.

By late October, after the first of several rains had descended upon the island, she sent word that heavy clothing was now needed again to prepare the homeless for winter. Last, she was absolutely determined to see donations from building suppliers, lumbermen, and contractors to build homes for the eight thousand homeless still living in tents or makeshift houses.

As a result of Barton's appeals, donations came from all parts of the United States and in all types and sizes. From an individual in San Antonio came twenty-five cents; Lizzie Stewart of Greensboro, North Carolina, sent her two-dollar "mite." From Dansville, New York, came 180 pounds of wheat. Two portable hospitals arrived from Chicago and were immediately put to use. A "little band of Red Cross girls" from Sharon, Pennsylvania, sent clothing, as did countless ladies' aid societies, churches, and needle craft guilds. The Epworth League of Miles, Iowa, and the "working people" of Long Beach, Mississippi, sent twenty-three and twelve dollars, respectively. Children in the public schools of Cottonwood Falls, Kansas, sent twenty dollars. Seven hens arrived from Edna, Texas, along with medical supplies from New York and New Orleans. Barrels and boxes full of clothing came from Worcester, Massachusetts; Flagstaff, Arizona; San Rafael, California; Algiers, Louisiana; and Sherman, Texas. The railroads and the Mallory Shipping Line carried all these supplies free of freight charges.

Businesses and laborers donated generously: from the E. B. Warren Co. in Washington, D.C., came 2,840 pounds of lime for disinfecting. The Pillsbury Company of Minnesota consigned to the Red Cross three railcar loads of flour. On September 24 two competing newspapers, the New York *World* and the New York *Journal*, sent seventy-five alcohol stoves. Lobdell and Percy, Jobbers and Manufacturers' Agents of Thibodaux, Louisiana, sent $165.00. From the Lumbermen's Exchange of Philadelphia came a check for $325.50 to help with building materials. Workers at the Cambria Steel Company in Johnstown, Pennsylvania, collected sixty-one dollars for relief. This brought a heartfelt reply from Barton, who found it "touching" that they should reach out to help victims of this flood, particularly since in 1889, Johnstown had been helped by the Red Cross after its own disastrous flood. The masters and crews of twelve steamships in Galveston harbor donated over five hundred dollars, which brought a personal reply from Barton, in which she stated, "It is only one more evidence of the great good will which has always been manifested between the shipping department and the Red Cross showing their intellectual knowledge of a great world beneficence and the ready heart of the sailor for the woes of others." The overall effect of the Red Cross appeals was substantial: 1,552 cases, 258 barrels, 542 packages, and 13 casks of clothing, bedding, shoes, crockery, groceries, disinfectants, medical supplies, and hardware came to its warehouse for distribution. Monetary donations sent to the Red Cross at work in Galveston amounted to $17,341; estimates of total donations in money, goods, and services came in at $120,000.

By September 20, Clara Barton was ready to inform Mayor Jones that the Red Cross had established its warehouse and had received its first shipment of relief supplies, with more to come. She stated that it was their desire "to make distribution or disposition of these supplies in such manner as shall accomplish the greatest degree of relief and only in accordance with the method being pursued by your committees." While being duly respectful of the existing relief structure, she hastened to add that the mayor and his relief committees should devise "some proper method whereby we may know all persons who are needy and worthy of our relief." This prompted a "grand meeting" between the city's emergency committees and the Red Cross staff in which Stephen Barton served as spokesperson. According to Clara Barton, the Red Cross

then merged fully into the existing relief structure, with representatives serving ex-officio on every existing committee. At that point the CRC transferred to the Red Cross the entire work of distributing food, clothing, and other relief supplies.

On the 23rd of September, Clara Barton and her nephew organized the staff, giving each their assignments: Fred Ward to supervise the warehouse, to be responsible for the receipt and delivery of all Red Cross goods, to keep financial records as well as accounts of the supplies received and distributed, and each week to prepare a statement for CRC relief chairman McVitie of approximate quantities and kinds of supplies delivered. Fannie B. Ward, Howard Tallmadge, and J. A. McDowell were to work as his assistants. H. W. Lewis was given charge of the Red Cross orphan asylum, of caring for the children and their lodging, and preparing food for those who were quartered in the warehouse. Within days boxes and barrels had been unpacked and sorted according to men's, women's, and children's clothing and shoes; and bedding and household items for the needy. Workers "fitted up temporary beds and a large kitchen in the warehouse" because eight or ten of the Red Cross representatives as well as the arriving orphans were lodged there. Most of the goods, however, were distributed to ward relief stations throughout the city. But the warehouse remained a focal point of activity from 6 A.M. until 10 P.M. every day until it closed October 31.

Clara Barton's humanitarian work and the energy of the women Red Cross workers inspired women leaders of Galveston also to become active agents of relief. On September 25 the Galveston *Daily News* noted that "a number of ladies met yesterday at the headquarters of the Red Cross society, on Twenty-fifth and Mechanic streets, to assist in the distribution of stores sent through that organization to the Galveston flood sufferers." Twenty-six white women leaders gathered to assist in the crisis. Barton quickly seized the opportunity to create Galveston Red Cross Auxiliary No. 1, honoring the city under a newly passed congressional provision that granted auxiliary status to branches. She wrote in her report: "The ladies of the city, inspite of the shock, grief, and mutilated homes, came grandly to the work of relief, asking to form a Red Cross auxiliary and take charge of the distributing stations in the various wards of the city, under the name of the Red Cross."

From the beginning, the relief committee under the leadership of William A. McVitie had devised a central commissary at 20th Street and the Strand to supply a system of relief stations. There was one station in each ward, with each chaired by a man.

The meeting of Barton, her workers, and city leadership made it clear that the Red Cross would step into the administration and distribution of relief materials. Galveston women, through their newly devised auxiliary, provided the leadership necessary to take over ward relief stations. The American National Red Cross supplied the twelve wards with relief goods as materials came to the central Red Cross warehouse. Giving in to the inevitable on September 27, the relief committee and the Red Cross "amalgamated"—a "lady chairman in each ward, [and] the gentlemen chairmen of the wards who have been working under the relief committee . . . to continue their good work," reported the *Daily News*. McVitie wanted the women to "predominate" because, he stated, they could "do this work better than the men." While women may have had more experience in such acts of charity, McVitie also arranged for them to work as volunteers, thus reducing expenses for the committee. Altogether 150 women and 50 men served in ward relief stations.

Volunteers distributed food, clothing, and materials for temporary shelters. Women went out among the people of their assigned wards to determine losses and then compiled a census, so that those who had specific needs, such as a stove or bedding, could be found and helped. Huge quantities of supplies poured into the city and the massive task of sorting, labeling, and distributing continued until the end of October. Barton praised the women for their work: "The best ladies of the city are heart and hand in them; they are diligently canvassing the town through all its wards to see personally after the needs of the sufferers."

One of the darkest tragedies to befall the city was the deaths of ninety children and ten Sisters from St. Mary's Orphan Asylum

FIGURE 2.15: The relief committee, under the leadership of William A. McVitie, devised a central commissary at 20th Street and the Strand, shown here, to supply a system of relief stations, one in each ward. (Courtesy Prints and Photographs Division, Library of Congress, Washington, D.C.)

and at least forty-seven children and six adults from the Home for Homeless Children and from Holy Rosary Home for Colored Children. More fortunate were fifty orphans and their attendants housed in the Galveston Orphans' Home, all of whom were spared, although the home was heavily damaged. They were sent out of the city until the building could be repaired. The plight of orphans and of children orphaned by the storm captured the hearts of donors outside the state. When Clara Barton and the Red Cross had arrived, they expected to find hundreds of orphans wandering the streets in need of homes. After her arrival, she informed the mayor that the Red Cross had opened a temporary residence "to receive and care for all of the orphans or destitute children, consequent upon the recent storm," and she implored the mayor to help supply information as to how many children were in need and where they might be found. Many orphans had already been removed to Houston or elsewhere; the Red Cross warehouse provided shelter for those children who remained. By October about twenty-one children occupied the entire second floor of the warehouse, their lodgings furnished with usable items from the damaged Galveston Orphans' Home. According to Clara Barton, they were taught by a kindergarten teacher who was "with them each day singing cheerily at their meals. . . ."

Newspaperman William Randolph Hearst, an ardent supporter of Barton and the Red Cross, also made plans to help Galveston's orphans. He sent a committee from the New York *Journal* to recruit the energetic Mrs. Roger A. Pryor to plan a three-day fundraising bazaar to be held in New York City. Undaunted by the fact that she had only three weeks to get the job done, Sarah Agnes Rice Pryor consented at once and began solicitations. So many offers for assistance poured in that she was forced to expand her office and choose a raft of volunteer assistants. Seeking social stars of the highest caliber, she began by requesting the endorsement of Queen Victoria of Great Britain (her majesty commanded that her sympathies be made known), the Duchess and the Dowager Duchess of Marlborough, the Baroness Burdett-Coutts, Lady Somerset, Lady Aberdeen, and Madame Díaz (wife of the Mexican

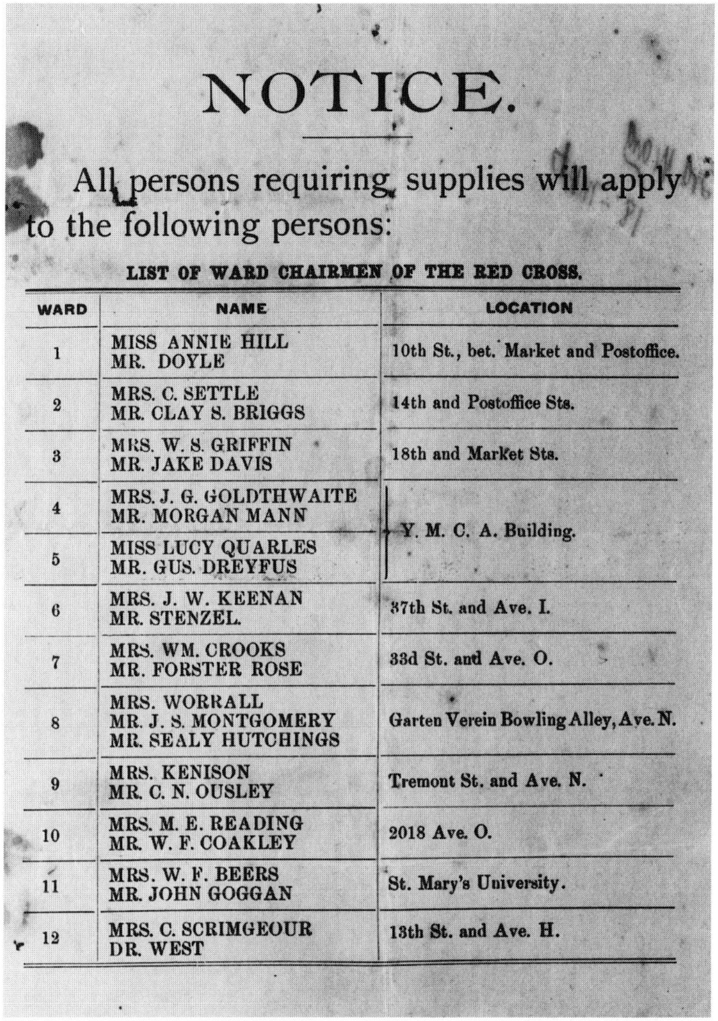

NOTICE.

All persons requiring supplies will apply to the following persons:

LIST OF WARD CHAIRMEN OF THE RED CROSS.

WARD	NAME	LOCATION
1	MISS ANNIE HILL MR. DOYLE	10th St., bet. Market and Postoffice.
2	MRS. C. SETTLE MR. CLAY S. BRIGGS	14th and Postoffice Sts.
3	MRS. W. S. GRIFFIN MR. JAKE DAVIS	18th and Market Sts.
4	MRS. J. G. GOLDTHWAITE MR. MORGAN MANN	Y. M. C. A. Building.
5	MISS LUCY QUARLES MR. GUS. DREYFUS	
6	MRS. J. W. KEENAN MR. STENZEL	37th St. and Ave. I.
7	MRS. WM. CROOKS MR. FORSTER ROSE	33d St. and Ave. O.
8	MRS. WORRALL MR. J. S. MONTGOMERY MR. SEALY HUTCHINGS	Garten Verein Bowling Alley, Ave. N.
9	MRS. KENISON MR. C. N. OUSLEY	Tremont St. and Ave. N.
10	MRS. M. E. READING MR. W. F. COAKLEY	2018 Ave. O.
11	MRS. W. F. BEERS MR. JOHN GOGGAN	St. Mary's University.
12	MRS. C. SCRIMGEOUR DR. WEST	13th St. and Ave. H.

FIGURE 2.16: On September 27, the relief committee and the Red Cross amalgamated to allow a Galveston woman to co-chair each ward for the distribution of relief goods. Clara Barton had made it possible for women volunteers to become integral to the relief operations, thus opening the door to their civic leadership. Altogether 150 women and 50 men served in ward relief stations. (Courtesy Rosenberg Library, Galveston, Texas.)

president). Once Sarah Pryor had secured her international line-up, she began working on New York high society, among them Mrs. Stuyvesant Fish, Mrs. Joseph Choate, and Mrs. John Jacob Astor. They too complied, and New York merchants fell all over themselves for the chance to give something of value to the bazaar. "Rich furs, tiger rugs, opera-cloaks, ladies' hats, silverware, watches, jewels, bicycles, a grand piano, and an automobile" were among the treasures sold for the Galveston orphans. Three thousand people attended the October gala event at the Waldorf Astoria hotel ballroom. Over the course of the three days, they heard Texas governor Joseph D. Sayers describe the calamity that had befallen the state's wealthiest city and the urgent needs of "the homeless orphans of Galveston." On the third evening Mark Twain entertained the guests, and the bazaar raised over fifty thousand dollars for the repair of the Galveston Orphans' Home, which was finally rededicated March 30, 1902.

When the Red Cross finished its mission in Galveston, it found homes for the children who had come to live in the warehouse. Seven months later the CRC reported that it had distributed $15,000 to St. Mary's Orphan Asylum; $10,000 to the Galveston Orphans' Home; $15,000 to the Home for Homeless Children; and $1,000 to Holy Rosary School and Home for Colored Orphans. Exclusion of blacks from the Central Relief Committee and the city council contributed to disparities in funding between black and white orphan asylums. Without a powerful voice in the relief structures, blacks received fewer funds for their dependents. There were no elaborate fund raisers for African American orphans, nor did the city fathers seem to sense that black children were just as vulnerable as white children.

Families who had lost their homes coped as best they could in the days after the storm. Many stayed on in their places of refuge, because their homes were destroyed and they had no place else to go. Ellen Mussey, a Red Cross worker, came across two black families living in the courtrooms of the mildly damaged courthouse. Others camped in damaged schools, churches, convents, and hospitals. The Karbowskis, a family of eight, miraculously survived in the shelter of Saint Mary's Catholic Seminary, but their rented house at the intersection of 9th Street and Avenue I had been demolished. That family spent the next night in a cottage with forty other people. Eventually they found another house to rent.

Louisa Rollfing escaped total disaster during the storm by fleeing with her children to the home of her sister-in-law. When the family reunited—and they were among the lucky ones—August, her husband, went to look for the place they had called home. It was completely gone. The family stayed with his mother immediately after the storm. Her house, still standing, was full of the residue from the sea, a dark scum that covered walls, bedding, and furnishings and took scrubbing to remove. Lack of fresh water made cleaning impossible; the family took mattresses and upholstered furniture outdoors to dry, but the terrible odor remained.

Because it was too difficult to stay in a house with such limited amenities, after ten days Louisa and the children left for Lake Charles, Louisiana, to stay with relatives. August had salvaged Louisa's trunk full of wet winter clothes, and she used these and a few purchases from depleted stores to put together travel outfits for herself and the children. She also bought a bolt of maroon cloth with tiny white flowers, and, upon arriving in Lake Charles, "started sewing as fast as I could." She made dresses for the girls and shirts and pants for the boy, shirtwaists for herself, petticoats, and underwear, all out of the same fabric. "I got tired of looking at red," she wrote later.

After a month, they returned to Galveston, but housing was in such short supply that the family lived in August Rollfing's workshop for ten days, sleeping on cots, eating meals from a gasoline stove, "and the children almost living in the street." At last she heard that two rooms over a grocery store were for rent at 37th Street and Avenue N. She took August's horse and gig—a perilous ride for her—and secured the rooms. They had so few belongings to move—cot, mattress, packing box, stove, trunk, box of dishes newly bought, and their dog Dewey, rescued from the storm—that the movers charged them only fifty cents. She used her winter clothing for curtains, and a friend gave them a case for the dishes

FIGURE 2.17: Despite the debris, life resumed for many residents, as shown by this woman toting a satchel of clothing, possibly laundry, in an opened passageway looking north on 19th Street. (Courtesy Prints and Photographs Division, Library of Congress, Washington, D.C.)

and a table without chairs so "at least we could stand around the table to eat." Thus did one family cope in the aftermath of the storm.

Some families scavenged planks and boards that lay about the island and constructed for themselves "storm lumber" houses. Others chose to live in their dilapidated homes, hoping for aid in repairs, while still others acquired one of the one thousand tents sent to the city and installed them on their own denuded lots. For workmen who came to help rebuild and for renters without hous-

ing, the "White City on the Beach," a temporary compound of two hundred tents that housed several hundred families, offered shelter.

This beach city extended from the east end of the island to 25th Street and was situated in the area swept clean of houses by the storm, south of the great mound of debris. The army sent the bulk of the tents—remnants from the Spanish-American War and some from the Civil War—and survivors improved them by building floors and appropriating furniture (some of it their own) from the wreckage.

FIGURE 2.18: Many families resorted to building their own storm lumber houses from the debris. The storm left ten thousand homeless. (Courtesy Prints and Photographs Division, Library of Congress, Washington, D.C.)

FIGURE 2.19: While the homeless lived in tents like this, Clara Barton insisted that the city move to construct sturdy housing before the onset of winter. She made a national appeal for lumber, roofing, hardware, tools, and other materials necessary to build new homes. (Courtesy Rosenberg Library, Galveston, Texas.)

FIGURE 2.20: The "White City on the Beach," a temporary compound of two hundred tents, extended from the east end of the island to 25th Street and was situated in the area swept clean of structures. It housed several hundred homeless families as well as workmen who had come to help rebuild the city. The army sent the bulk of the tents—remnants from the Spanish-American War, and some from the Civil War. (Courtesy Prints and Photographs Division, Library of Congress, Washington, D.C.)

At the foot of 23rd Street (Tremont), the relief committee erected hospital tents, kitchen tents, and a dining room with prepared meals that was supervised by Rabbi Henry Cohen. The *Daily News* called the city "the most healthful and in the best sanitary condition of any place on the island. It is situated south of the foul smelling debris and is exposed to the purifying elements of the salt south breeze." Advertising as if it were a health resort, the *Daily News* mentioned vacancies and predicted that the settlement would grow rapidly. This brought an immediate rebuke, polite, of course, from Clara Barton, who saw the tent city as a danger to the future of the homeless.

By late September the problem of shelter had become a constant worry. Sensing the need for action before winter closed in, Barton began a letter-writing campaign to Red Cross supporters to begin directing money into building materials for the homeless. The hungry, the ragged, and the orphaned were now cared for, she wrote, "but there are 8,000 homeless people. Where shall these wretched people go? . . . Many owned their homes; but for miles and miles along the coast even the ground is gone and the restless tide ebbs and flows over what was all to them . . ." By September 30 she had dashed off a letter (published in the Galveston *Daily News* October 2) to Bertrand Adoue, chairman of the committee on the reconstruction of homes, "urging the importance of the immediate adoption of some fixed plan of action by yourselves, so that a definite statement can be made to the American people of your wants in this most important direction." She continued, "I believe a computation should be made showing the maximum estimated number of homeless people, including those who are now within the city and those who have sought shelter and asylum outside and who would return if any accommodations offered. . . ." Let the American people know how many houses, no matter how modest, the reconstruction committee planned to provide, she lectured. "Our experience teaches us that it is only necessary to inform the public in a business-like way the exact needs . . . and the efforts will at once be earnestly directed in such channels." Have the architects plan to rebuild "in a definite and comprehensive

way." She also suggested an appeal be made for lumber, roofing, hardware, tools, and other materials necessary, including furniture, kitchen utensils, and bedding. Miles and miles of debris, splintered and water damaged, was of little use for the building of new homes and had to be burned or carted away to the mainland.

Such forceful and authoritative words from a woman may well have shocked the relief committeemen, but if the male leaders of Galveston resented hearing directives from Clara Barton, they made no public complaint. And if she felt that they neglected the needs of the homeless, she made no public acknowledgment either. In a letter to President William McKinley, she praised the Galveston leaders, who were "destroyed in business, crippled in finances, but on whom must fall the great final burden of relief. My respect for these men increases with every day's meetings. I have never seen such unanimity of action. No discord, nor self-thought, but one settled, united purpose. . . ." Then she let President McKinley know that restoring shelter was the great pressing need. She demurely noted that the "perplexed Committee has called us into consultation." Clara Barton established in Galveston a commanding female presence. Her demeanor must have also come as a revelation to women volunteers working in ward commissaries. Moral authority, pronounced by a respectable woman, held weight. This would become a valuable tool for future women activists.

The building committee was under the leadership of Bertrand Adoue and Morris Lasker—both influential businessmen who felt it would be wise to include a representative of Galveston's labor unions. In October, they invited William V. McConn, editor of the Galveston *Journal*, labor's official organ, to join the committee. McConn was the only person to represent organized labor on the CRC, and his inclusion meant that the workmen who participated in the reconstruction of the island finally had a voice among the city's leaders. The committee did as instructed; it made its accounting, and Clara Barton sent out the appeal to the "Manufacturers of and Dealers in, Lumber, Hardware, Builders Materials and Household Goods and to the Business Men in General of the

United States." It listed specific needs for lumber, bricks, door frames, hinges, roofing, and household furnishings. Although she accepted her role as a complement to the efforts of the city leaders, she nonetheless felt they needed to see the larger picture, to prepare for the "rehabilitation" phase of relief work. In a confessional to her friend, William Howard, she opined, "I believe so far in the good heartedness of the people and the good sense of its business men as to think they will in measure adopt and conform to the plans we have given."

By October 11, the Shreveport *Times* let her know that lumber mills in that state were readying to send shipments. And with a letter of introduction from Clara Barton in hand, Morris Lasker headed for New York to raise money for new homes. At the same time that Lasker's appeal went out, a group of Texas women living in Washington, D.C., organized Red Cross Auxiliary No. 3 to raise money for housing. With the endorsement of Congressman R. B. Hawley from Galveston, they held a fund raiser in the largest theater in Washington, with prominent speakers and a Marine band. The fund raiser and other donations netted seventeen hundred dollars for use by the building committee.

The tasks of the building committee were daunting. It received five thousand applications for assistance from people living in roofless, windowless, damaged homes or from those whose homes were completely destroyed. Materials and workmen were scarce, and the needs of property owners were great. Although others on the island suggested building temporary tenements, the committee went with Barton's plan for constructing individual homes and helping to pay for the repair of damaged ones. It spent $450,000 on this reconstruction project. (This did not include donations sent in response to Clara Barton's appeal to the building industry.) The committee appointed four inspectors to evaluate each applicant's needs and determine a monetary contribution for damaged homes; in cases where the house had been completely destroyed, it contracted with builders to erect a three-room cottage. To the committee's credit, it did not discriminate between the races.

At first the committee hired any live body willing to build

houses, but the results were terrible and 90 percent of the cottages had to be rebuilt. When William V. McConn joined the building committee, he convinced the others that union labor was needed to construct these homes. He was able to see his trade-union colleague, T. W. Dee, appointed to the inspection team. When the committee adopted the plan to secure union labor, it allowed the building tradesmen to have a hand in the city's project, and the results were good for city leaders. Labor unions felt included in the post-storm recovery; they benefited from the city's largest contract; and they became supporters of Galveston's elite leadership. All of this would have tremendous ramifications for the creation of the city commission form of government, which relied on labor's support to succeed.

Best of all to the occupants, their work was sound. They completed nearly 80 percent of the structures, with fewer repairs necessary, and at a lower cost to the city. The 483 houses that were built cost between $300 and $350 each. Most of these were three-rooms-in-a-row wooden shotgun houses with clapboard siding. Galvestonians called them "commissary" houses probably because they were issued like relief goods from the ward commissaries.

For owners who were willing to donate their labor or some supplies, the committee spent about $265 a piece on average to rebuild some 1,100 homes. Owners needing repairs—approximately 1,114—received cash payments of between $16 and $359. Renters were least likely to see their former homes repaired or rebuilt quickly, since the committee favored owners, and owners often concentrated on their own homes and not their renters'. Even so, the need for construction workers was so great and the business so heavy that delays of weeks were not unusual. Real estate agent H. M. Trueheart reported to an absentee landlord in Chicago that "It will be sometime before we can get an estimate as to what it will cost to repair them [rental houses], as it is almost impossible to get mechanics. It is estimated that 97 $^{1}/_{2}$ per cent of all the houses in the city have been more or less damaged by the storm." Thus the system of disbursement rewarded property owners rather than the propertyless, compounding the latter's insecurity after the tragedy and forcing them to rely on relief long after property owners had begun to reestablish themselves.

Besides relief and rebuilding, maintaining public health challenged those remaining on the island. Citizens faced the daunting task of cleaning and restoring their homes and businesses. J. H. Hawley complained bitterly to his family that

the storm has left the city without drainage and the limited supply of water prevents us from giving much attention at present to our sanitary condition. The wreckage I have referred to is fully 100 feet deep and in many places 25 feet high, . . . Of course you understand the accumulation of filth etc., the stench, arising from the lack of drainage from perhaps 40,000 people, must produce sanitary conditions injurious to the health in the last degree. The weather is intensely hot, since the 8th of Sep't to the present time [September 18]. The weather has been perfectly clear and with the sun beating down on it, odors arise making it most unbearable.

The Central Relief Committee was so concerned about cleanliness and the outbreak of disease in the wake of the storm that it invited New York City sanitation expert Dr. George A. Soper to counsel them. After a thorough inspection of the city, he proclaimed, "Your city is very unsanitary." He was critical of the inadequate sewerage system and hoped that a better one would be installed. Continue the cremation of bodies and the disposal of debris, advised Soper, but

put [the city] in a very clean condition. The gutters and the alleys in which liquid filth has accumulated should be thoroughly cleaned out and disinfected. . . . Streets should be cleaned by sweeping and carrying away the matter collected, . . . the privies and stables should be looked after and . . . the sewers should be investigated to see that they are in working condition. . . .

"The danger, he said, was "not from the dead but from those living in crowded conditions." Soper suggested that a larger team of men be employed to work in the city health department, which was understaffed with only twenty men. This was done, with Soper and Dr. C. H. Wilkinson, city health officer, in charge of "the entire sanitary work, both on the streets and private property." The city health department and the CRC distributed free disinfectants through the ward "disinfectant depot" and sent garbage collectors with carts to remove trash and debris placed in barrels outside of homes and in alleys. Inspectors came to every house. Citizens who did not dispose of their trash properly were cited or taken to court and fined; the judge did not accept excuses that claimed defendants were "too busy making a living."

But making a living did consume the energies of those who intended to remain on the island. If trading houses, the port, factories, and the livelihoods of artisans could not be restored, Galveston would die, and all the efforts to feed supplicants, restore housing, and clean the city would be in vain.

Signs of life on the Strand, the commercial emporium of Texas, appeared immediately. Less severely damaged than structures on the Gulf side of the island, the Strand reopened for business as soon as merchants put their stores in order. Salvageable damaged goods were offered at reduced prices. Wholesale grocers Pabst and Leinback sold "surprise" canned goods without their labels. Downtown streets bloomed with drying carpets, curtains, and bolts of yardage, hanging from lines in front of stores like some immense laundry load.

Before long, city services resumed. By Wednesday, September 12, the first mail came in by boat—to be retrieved from the post office since home delivery was impossible—and it was not long before the island's utilities were restored. Through nonstop efforts of carpenters and engineers, water was restored to the city's pumping plant and into the water mains by Thursday. Those without damaged pipes received water. On September 13, Western Union employees strung a wire atop pilings of the bay bridge and restored one line between Galveston and Houston. This was used mostly by the military officers guarding the island and by relief committee requests—for which the company charged no fee. But several days

FIGURE 2.21: Like an immense laundry load, merchants hung their wet goods out to dry along the Strand. They were open for business as soon as their wares could be salvaged. (Courtesy Prints and Photographs Division, Library of Congress, Washington, D.C.)

later, with a force of 130 men, Western Union quadrupled the service, until it was able to lay a new submarine cable ordered from Chicago on the floor of the bay. The Galveston *Daily News* resumed publishing a full-sized paper, although it had not missed a single day since the storm.

On Friday the banks opened, and real estate transactions resumed. A lot and house sold for three thousand dollars. Saturday, mule-drawn streetcars were again running from Avenue D (Market) to 21st Street to Broadway to 40th Street and back. Electric lights returned to streets and stores; the brewery and the ice plant reopened.

On Sunday, September 16, the front page of the *Daily News* bristled with notices from merchants, bankers, cotton factors, and roofers that they were, or soon would be, open for business. Those houses of worship still standing hosted services for their own and for others. Christian Scientists opened their doors to other worshipers; members of the African American St. Augustine Episcopal Church met in Eaton Chapel, salvaged from the ruins of Trinity Episcopal Church; Methodists went to the Central Christian Church; and members of First Baptist and several other churches worshiped in the Jewish synagogue. Martha Poole, a Baptist, remembers with gratitude the beneficence of Temple B'nai Israel. "The awful storm of 1900 swept away all our church buildings and 50 of our members. . . . We were in despair, but God helped us. Our neighbors, the Jews, opened the doors of the synagogue to us, like genuine Christians; although their building was greatly damaged. I changed my seat there four times one Sunday, to escape a wetting."

On Monday, September 17, the day the Red Cross arrived, long-distance telephone service returned. By Friday of the second week workmen had cleared the streets for traffic, laid underground telephone lines, and repaired one railroad bridge for joint use across the bay. The first Santa Fe train came whistling in at 6:20 A.M. That same day, martial law ended, and, in a leap of faith, the saloons were reopened.

There were plenty of jobs for skilled carpenters and construc-

tion workers, especially on the wharves, which had sustained enormous damage. When George Sealy, president of the Galveston Wharf Company, first surveyed the wreckage, he "broke down and for a moment cried like a child." But the deep water channel remained, and, with hearty optimism, the Galveston Wharf Company hired hundreds of men to repair the broken wharves and warehouses. Ben Stuart reported that the Southern Pacific Railroad would rebuild its piers to connect with the Morgan Steamship Line, and three weeks after the storm, Galveston handled its first load of cotton since the storm. Six weeks after the hurricane, ships were plying in and out of a harbor rapidly under construction. The Galveston *Tribune* painted a triumphant picture:

From Tenth Street . . . to 35th Street on the west, the bay front is lined with great ocean steamships. . . . In one slip six mighty ocean carriers with a total capacity of nearly one hundred thousand bales of cotton are clustered. The sound of the steam hoist dragging the great bales aboard, the heave of the "cotton-jammer" as he screws the packages into the smallest space possible in the vessel's hold, the rattle of the hand truck as the "gobbler" comes rolling the bales to the slings, the rumble of the drays bringing loads of oil-cake, flour and other cargo from car to shipside, the puffing of the locomotives and the crashing of the cars as they are switched in and out of the great long piers, makes noise enough to wake the dead; but commingled with these sounds are the raspings of many hundreds of saws and the sharp crack, rack-dack of hundreds of hammers telling the story of the army of builders, who, without interfering with the regiments of wharfmen handling the cargoes, are restoring the immense sheds, rebuilding the piers and the wharves where the storm ravaged them, and making better and stronger the whole dockage and wharfage system of the port.

Businessmen and laborers knew that the city was on the road to recovery when 30,300 bales of cotton left the port on October 14.

By October 22 four white schools and one African American school reopened. Schools had suffered extensive damage and the question had been what to do with children when the semester began. The situation was severe for white children, but it was even more dire for blacks. African Americans had attended three schools in Galveston; one of them, East District School, was completely destroyed, and Central High School for black students was so damaged that classes could not be held for months. In addition, seven teachers out of a total of twenty-three had drowned. Pupils from all the segregated black schools squeezed into the only safe building—the small West District Elementary School on 35th Street. Almost a year later parents were still complaining to white school board trustees that East District school remained closed. Of course, money was the issue. Superintendent John W. Hopkins had directed a public subscription campaign which raised eighty thousand dollars, not enough to fund all reconstruction in one year.

Twenty days after the storm, a plea had gone out from the board of trustees of the Galveston schools to the New York City Board of Education asking the New Yorkers to take up a collection to help the children of Galveston. Such a request was a challenge for the eastern officials because they held to a strict policy prohibiting solicitation of school children. But for Galveston, the New York board made an exception. Teachers and students from every borough—Manhattan, the Bronx, Brooklyn, Queens, and Richmond (now Staten Island)—gave money. The majority gave one cent, but when the donations were counted, they totaled $27,907. Miles J. O'Brien, president of the New York Board of Education, sent a specially designed check—picturing happy schoolchildren—to the Galveston school board trustees January 6, 1901. School board president M. E. Kleberg responded with their "measureless gratitude" for children helping children in a national recovery effort.

Finally, on October 25, 1900, the ward relief stations closed, followed several days later by the Red Cross warehouse. On the 31st the industrious Red Cross workers shipped four railcar loads of goods to Houston to help the storm victims there, mainly farmers. The Red Cross orphanage was disassembled, and the orphans sent to live with relatives or with new families. With the remaining

funds Clara Barton ordered seed, fertilizers, grain for animals, provisions, and a million and a half strawberry plants from North Carolina, Illinois, Arkansas, and Louisiana to be distributed to the mainland farmers whose crops would bloom by December and be edible by early spring. Having left the impoverished with something to start anew, Barton departed Galveston for Washington, D.C., on November 15. Her reward came in March when she and her staff enjoyed a basket of the ripened berries sent from Texas. Galveston was well on its way to recovery.

Heroism knows no race. At the height of the storm and after in the grueling days of funerary detail, African Americans proved this truism. Writers at the time observed a curious phenomenon that in the midst of the crisis, in this southern city where most institutions were segregated, race did not seem to matter. Saving lives did. Daniel Ransom, mentioned earlier, put the lives of others before his own. Henry Johnson, a black workman, noticed that among the rescuers in his neighborhood everyone was treated alike. When they reached the train station, "white people and colored people [were] all bundled up . . . together." Tales of black refugees singing in the sanctuary of Ursuline Convent or huddled at the Union Passenger station attest to a certain human commonality among all storm sufferers.

There is much to admire in the tales of heroism and sacrifice from people of both races, but the emergency mentality that brought blacks and whites together did not survive the disaster. Attitudes of white superiority and fear of black unruliness in the face of danger or want had a historic hold on the city's white citizens. As soon as the waters receded and the sun shone on a devastated island, old patterns of race relations reasserted themselves, sometimes in surprisingly harsh ways.

Reports of scavengers, looters, and robbers of the dead were heard at the initial meetings of the CRC. At first race was not mentioned, but in the few days before troops arrived and martial law was imposed, race emerged as an issue. Indications that prejudice clouded the picture, however, came when reports identified blacks as looting, stealing, or acting as "ghouls" by cutting off fingers for jewelry and ransacking the pockets of the dead. Volunteers from the Screwmen's Benevolent Association, who were given leave to patrol the streets, were instructed that their mission was to "protect the negroes from robbing the dead"—with the obvious implication that whites were expecting blacks to steal. Letters from survivors to those outside the city show that they identified stealing with race; Louisa Rollfing blamed "niggers" for taking part of her husband's clothes from a trunk their neighbors had recovered. Others wrote that "ghouls"—more often than not, meaning blacks—were killed on the spot. Anna Focke wrote her daughters in Germany that "ears and hands have been cut off the dead, because of ear-rings and rings. Fingers have been found in the pockets of looters, mostly Negroes, one of whom had sixteen and another eleven." The Galveston *Daily News* reported on September 12 that "Quite a number of negroes were killed for looting" by deputized patrollers. Henry Wolfram thought that as many as forty-five were shot and killed. Sensationalist authors, who flooded the country with books on the hurricane, raised the numbers to seventy-five, again with a racial implication. Published pen-and-ink drawings, showing black figures skulking about the debris and the visible dead bodies, brought the rumors to life. Even the staid Chicago *Tribune* reported that twenty-four negroes were shot while pillaging wrecked homes and that several guardsmen were killed in the fracas. Harper's *Weekly* estimated that "hundreds" of vicious types, "many of them negroes, were as diligent in evil work as the rescuers were in good."

Contrasts of good and evil often were understood as white and black. Clarence Ousley, who investigated the rumors and innuendoes, could find no evidence that more than six people were summarily executed for stealing from the dead, and it is more probable, according to police reports, that arrests for robbing bodies and looting came to eight, with race unknown and unrecorded. No reports of executions can be found in police records for September and October, but one must remember that the police were not the only armed men guarding the island. As a result of a *Daily News* story that eight negroes had been shot for looting, Governor Sayers urged caution and restraint to law enforcers. No doubt the governor saw the advent of General Scurry and the Texas militia men as a way to end indiscriminate shooting of suspected blacks. Scurry, however, turned out to be no friend to African Americans.

In the days following the storm, one can only try to imagine the chaos and disorder that reigned—debris and bodies everywhere, quantities of food and water unknown, utilities wrecked, transportation cut off, little shelter for the homeless, and too few policemen to prevent stealing or to oversee efforts to remove bodies and rubble. In this highly charged atmosphere, white fears of blacks—fed by racial stereotypes—surfaced and shaped the post-storm recovery.

The specter of black criminal behavior was accompanied by assumptions that, unless forced, blacks would not work. The Galveston *Daily News* reported: "It was decided to take the bodies to sea, . . . But men refused to touch the bodies. This was especially true of the negroes. . . . Men were impressed at the point of a bayonet to do the work that must be done." White supervisors forced at gun point a gang of fifty black men to accompany the dead on the barges headed out to sea for burial. Did the men really have to be forced? One wonders, considering that in the first call for crews hired to clear debris from Tremont Street, fourteen of the twenty-five recruits were black. Members of both the white Screwmen's Benevolent Association and the black Cotton Jammers' Association, all of whom were dockworkers, volunteered to clear debris. In a rare concession to black sacrifices, the *Daily News* praised both labor organizations: "To the credit of the colored screwmen's organization let it be said that they followed the splendid example of their white brethren with gratuitous labor. . . ." Photographs show white and black work crews tackling the mess or burning bodies at cremation pyres. Yet the Chicago *Tribune*, rivaling white southerners in their prejudices, wrote that "many of the negroes who handle the bodies fell from fright and nausea. White volunteers took their places and the work went on."

Blacks were depicted as irresponsible, childish, and fearful, while whites were held to be manly and courageous. Galveston *Daily News* journalists wrote "Grewsome Stories" and derided a "colored man" for "drinking steadily" from a beer keg during the storm before being washed out with the tide. Another *Daily News* story of "an aged negro" who found his son while recovering bodies for cremation perhaps shows more sympathy, but it turns the man's pain into an example of weakness. The work crew offered to bury the boy while the man "cried like a child." Newspaper accounts and post-storm books mostly either vilified or infantilized African Americans while representing whites as models of stoicism, bravery, and efficiency.

There were some emergency leaders who were clearly more sympathetic to blacks but still held patronizing attitudes. Clarence Ousley of the *Daily News* authored *Galveston in 1900* as a corrective to highly sensationalized accounts that sold widely across the nation. His book did not vilify or infantilize blacks, but it often betrayed his condescension. Clara Barton was another who plainly cared about the welfare of black Galvestonians; she treated them with great kindness and yet she saw them as more pitiable and less self-reliant.

How did African Americans react? This question should be viewed against the backdrop of the African American community in Galveston, which by 1900 had emerged as insular but strong. Black citizens did not remain silent; they complained about discriminatory treatment in their newspaper and to the Red Cross. When white leaders excluded blacks from the CRC, they betrayed their prejudice. No black leaders, not even former aldermen, were invited to share in the decision making or to become ward representatives, although black leaders labored under white leadership or blacks led other blacks. The Reverend Frank Gary, for instance, pastor of St. Paul's Methodist Church, which was a black congregation, managed a gang of men who worked to remove debris from the East End. Laboring without representation at the highest levels rankled, however, as seen in this angry letter posted in the black-owned Galveston *City Times*:

The colored man is good enough to save the lives of the little white babes, white women and even men. Good enough to visit the sick, bury the dead, care for the helpless, and render noble assistance in every particular . . . and yet in all of that he has not been good enough to even be represented as a committeeman. He has lost everything he had and in two wards he was entitled to a committeeman.

FIGURE 2.22: This photograph of an African American survivor was originally a stereograph produced by M. H. Zahner, Publisher, Niagara Falls, New York. The caption read, "I'm glad I'se Living," indicating that stereotyping of blacks after the storm was not limited to southerners alone. (Courtesy Prints and Photographs Division, Library of Congress, Washington, D.C.)

As if to add to the insult, on September 14 an item appeared in the *Daily News* accusing working-class and African American women of fraud at the ward relief commissaries.

The ward relief committees are having a great deal of difficulty in distributing supplies to the people who require them. The supply depots are overrun with negroes and white women and children have the greatest difficulty in getting anywhere within range of the committees. It is said the negroes go from ward to ward and draw supplies at each depot as being a resident of each ward. Most of the negroes applying are women, and they inevitably claim that they have no husband, or that they have lost all relatives.

Four days later, complaints expanded to include working-class white women: "bad female characters, both white and black have been parading the streets and making themselves obnoxious." The CRC called General Scurry to impress and detain in a camp "all idle women found on the streets." The *Daily News* editors labeled the camp "particularly for negroes." They suggested that all destitute women should be fed in the camp and detained there so as to "prevent the practice of fraud by people in drawing rations. . . . Where women state they have no male members of their family they will be sent to the camp and kept there until they are willing to work at regular wages for private parties or the public." The motive for threatening black women with detention was revealed in the following *Daily News* item: "Many families are badly in need of help in the kitchen and household. When colored women are approached and asked if they want to work in many cases they ask exorbitant wages or refuse to work at any price. . . . They must either remain in the camp or go to work for private families or the public."

Incarcerating "troublesome" blacks was a solution borne of fear that black women were rebelling against the racial order by rushing in to receive goods and by refusing to work for whites. Scarcity in the face of great want often excites fears of riots and disorder that could lead to racial unrest. Better to imprison part of the population than to have rampant "fraud," no matter how great the need. This was justified on the grounds that these women would not work for wages. Distribution was the problem, but rather than admit difficulties in apportioning fairly the few goods available, the CRC called into play racial and class stereotyping. Several days later the *Daily News* reported that clothing donations had come to one of the Red Cross distribution centers. Ward volunteers—all white—gave away goods to whites in the morning and whatever was left over to blacks in the afternoon. Where blacks were accused of fraud, whites were guilty of discrimination and unequal distribution of donated items. This was too blatant for the black community to accept, and the Reverend W. A. Campbell lodged a complaint with the Red Cross that relief workers were guilty of gross inequities with regard to black supplicants. The Red Cross served as a neutral sounding board and even an advocate for blacks who suffered doubly—as aggrieved victims of both disaster and discrimination.

Clara Barton and the Red Cross workers took a kind but patronizing approach toward the Galveston African American community. As soon as possible Clara Barton contacted John R. Gibson, principal of Central High School, to form a "[Red Cross] society with all proper officers, seal, etc., and fit themselves to receive a little money." In response to the disaster, the African Americans from Beaufort, Port Royal, and Charleston, South Carolina, who themselves had been the recipients of Red Cross aid in the Sea Island Hurricane of 1893, sent over four hundred dollars in relief money to Galveston blacks, as did African Americans from Thibodaux, Louisiana, and from Alexandria, Virginia. Clara Barton ceremoniously presented this money to Gibson and his Red Cross volunteers, who later numbered twenty-six and formed the Red Cross Auxiliary. She reported that as they departed, "the moment seemed sacred when these poor, dark figures struggling toward the light walked out of my presence." The society spent very little of the money on relief, saving the bulk of the funds for a "Home for Indigent Colored People." For immediate relief, black

Red Cross members distributed clothing sent to them, 335 Bibles, and books for schoolchildren. Barton also

met the Delegation of the Old Colored Ladies' Home, only a few of whom remain and who fled in the storm heavenward to the Church steeple which alone stood, and in which they still stay. I arranged by the aid of the Jewish Rabbi [Cohen] to get them earthward; he giving them a tent, and I the stove and furniture and $20 to floor and make it comfortable. It might be interesting to know that the $20 were from a gift of the Port Royal storm sufferers, our old proteges.

Aside from these individual contributions, Barton made it clear to Gibson that blacks were entitled to the resources available in the ward distribution centers.

The policy of the Red Cross was to deal with everyone equally on the basis of need, but patterns of segregation at the turn of the century, particularly when emergencies occurred in the South, presented dilemmas for the organization. When Red Cross workers entered a disaster site, they acted cordially toward city leaders, offering to aid but not to supersede them in the application of relief. By channeling money earmarked for blacks to the newly formed African American Red Cross society under the supervision of principal Gibson, she escaped the issue of dealing with the all-white CRC, which might not have given the funds directly to the intended recipients. This avoided an open disagreement. Problems arose, however, when the policy of equal distribution clashed with that of segregation and discrimination. Clara Barton learned of problems when the Reverend W. A. Campbell came repeatedly to the Red Cross to discuss the manner of distribution of goods to African Americans in Galveston.

Reverend Campbell wrote an appeal to Barton in which he indicated that he trusted she could apply a remedy without a public protest. The problem was the unequal distribution of goods and the choosing of distributors. Apparently Campbell had initially been working in one of the ward relief stations but had been dismissed.

He wrote:

It is claimed, and, from observation, we hold, with some justice, that the colored people are not being equally dealt with by those who distribute the clothing at the several wards. Very often they are treated with such abruptness, that though in great straights, they do not return. Also the clothing is picked over, and the worst given them. We therefore suggest, that to stop any further complaint, on the days the clothing is to be issued to colored people, that a colored person of repute be appointed to distribute the same. There are several of the colored teachers who can be had to do this work; and also others who will willingly lend a hand. . . .

Reverend Campbell spoke also of the nature of the second-hand clothing distributed.

Many of them now being issued are unfit for wear. The man who opens the boxes in the Seventh ward stated to us that [many] of these were decidedly offensive. The question is shall we run the risk of generating the germs of disease, in this hot weather; and, subject ourselves to small pox, or some such pest that arises from just such uncleanness. These things are often given to the very poorest the worst class, into whose hand they can fall. For filth is then likely to be added to filth.

He added a list of names of those who could help with the distribution and suggested that a problem also existed with grocery distribution since "many worthy old people have complained of being turned off for unnecessary reasons."

That same day, Stephen Barton fired off a letter to Chairman William A. McVitie stating that Campbell had been to see him several times and had suggested that "colored teachers could better reach the colored people in the investigation of their wants and worthiness than any others . . ." and asked "that he may be permitted, or appointed in some way to serve with the Galveston Red Cross ladies in that capacity." On the matter of infected clothing,

Clara Barton wrote to suppliers—delicately—not to take any chances with the victims by sending adulterated goods, and implying that if there were an outbreak of diphtheria, they would all fear that perhaps diseased clothing had been the cause of it. The Bartons became important mediators between the black and the white communities.

The black community survived the year of recovery. Aid came through the Red Cross, the Central Relief Committee, and African American groups outside of Galveston. W. H. Noble, editor of the Galveston *City Times*, was the first to get the word out to the black press associations about the tremendous need. His appeal reached 150 black newspapers, and in response Cyrus F. Adams, president of the National Afro-American Press Association, authorized Noble to open a headquarters in the name of the association in order to receive donations. Noble directed all funds collected to John Sealy, chairman of the CRC finance committee, but he also advised civic leaders that "the colored people of this country can do much to assist in helping the suffering here . . . [they] are willing to do their part in every particular to show the people of the world that they are with Galveston in her hour of distress." Black men were hired to clean streets and clear debris at the same wages as whites; homes were eventually rebuilt or repaired, many with the help of the city's rebuilding committee; thirteen black churches stood at the end of the year; by 1902 the Negro Hospital was receiving patients; Holy Rosary Home for Colored Orphans took in more orphans from the storm; black laborers, dockworkers, businessmen, professionals, teachers, and preachers returned to work; and black children went back to school. But one aspect of life for African Americans that did not resume after the hurricane was participation in local politics.

African American men had lost ground politically as a result of laws to restrict voting at the state and local levels as early as 1895. With lack of representation in city government, African Americans then had no official voice to protect their interests or to remind white voters that all citizens deserved fair treatment and equal representation. Thus prejudice on the part of whites was reinforced by newspaper accounts and stories unfavorable to African Americans. When Galveston and other national newspapers reported that blacks were caught looting and robbing the dead or were seen as unmanly and uncourageous, it served to accelerate white distrust of an important portion of the community. Tension that developed in the aftermath of the storm led to increased discrimination against African Americans on the part of city leaders, the general public, and the white press, on the one hand, and increased sympathy on the part of clergy, the Red Cross, and some members of the city's white leadership on the other. But neither the heroism and sacrifices of African Americans, nor the character of men like Gibson, Campbell, and Noble held any sway with white voters when it came to endorsing a new form of city government. In the formative and fluid period between the storm and the triumph of the city commission, new civic leaders were being groomed for office holding, and it was clear that black men would not be included.

Ironically, just as black men and women found themselves pleading to be included in official relief circles and the object of unflattering reports, white women became the city's darlings. Traditional gender systems insisted that women remain guardians of the home and perhaps advocates for the poor, the orphaned, or the disabled; politics and public policy had always been reserved for men. Yet, men had acquiesced in partnering with women in the hard physical and psychological work of ward relief. The Galveston *Daily News* gave white women high praise for leaving their homes to work for the distressed in the city. Clara Barton and her female co-workers were models of charitable relief, but Galveston did not need an outside agency to see that women had been working for the good of dependents in the city for nearly thirty years. Still, just as the local press sent a negative message to readers about blacks, it also prepared Galveston readers for the "New Woman" who would move into realms of public policy making, beginning with public health. For white middle- and upper-class women, doors to politics opened, even if just an inch.

Prior to the presence of the American National Red Cross in

FIGURE 2.23: The Bath Avenue School, seen in the foreground, suffered more structural damage than the Letitia Rosenberg Women's Home, nearby. The Women's Home had been constructed and maintained by its Board of Lady Managers. After the storm, the board assumed responsibility for its repair. (Courtesy Rosenberg Library, Galveston, Texas.)

Galveston, white women had had very little opportunity to participate in official public policy roles. For thirty years, since the founding of the first women's immigrant aid, church, and synagogue societies, they had performed humanitarian tasks in what might be called a parallel civic structure. When in the 1880s and 1890s upper-middle-class white Protestant and Jewish women formed the Galveston Orphans' Home, the Letitia Rosenberg Women's Home, the Home for Homeless Children, and the Julia Runge Free Kindergarten, they acted as guardians and caretakers of the city's most vulnerable and dependent residents.

In this parallel civic structure, women assumed tasks of fund raising; hiring architects; approving plans; choosing contractors; hiring matrons, nurses, teachers, and assistants; admitting students and inmates (a term widely used in the nineteenth century to mean any person living in an asylum); adopting out orphans; and maintaining the institutions with money, time, organization, and energy. Male civic leaders praised women for their contributions to the city; yet, women could not vote. This meant that any favored policy change or implementation had to be achieved through persuasion rather than voting. Texas women did not gain the right to vote in primaries until 1918 or in general elections until 1920; thus electoral conditions for women after September 1900 did not change. What changed was their attitude toward and their access to public power.

After the storm, white and black women, separately, began to participate in the formation of public policy. Clara Barton had set the example. She was the only woman appointed to the powerful Central Relief Committee. She had organized twelve women to co-chair the ward relief stations, or commissaries, giving—for the first time—political appointments and official recognition from the CRC. Thus did male leaders include women in local government. Barton enlisted 150 women in the emergency relief efforts. And because she controlled access to substantial funds and goods, she was able to dictate an agenda for the construction of homes to a reconstruction committee that she believed was dragging its feet. She and the Red Cross workers willingly entered this city of doom, un-daunted by grisly deaths and the specter of disease and privation. Her courage inspired courage. Galveston women saw in their midst a powerful and effective woman humanitarian, who in no way "unsexed" herself by assuming a masculine demeanor. She demonstrated that a woman could lead and still be a woman. The emergency events held important consequences for women and for the city. Female response to the crisis provided a model for activism and led to the creation of the Women's Health Protective Association (WHPA) in 1901 and in 1914 a United Charities, which provided more systematic welfare relief under the direction of women administrators.

Directly and indirectly, white women civic leaders involved themselves in public policy decisions after the storm. One way was through informal connections that existed between wives, daughters, sisters, and mothers of the male members of the Deep Water Committee, the CRC, and the yet-to-be-formed city commission government. Many of these women had worked in the relief stations of the wards or had assumed leading positions in the Red Cross auxiliary. Personal connections to male leaders were important for the access to power that they afforded white women. The Women's Health Protective Association was another avenue for women to approach city leaders and implement policies. Many who had been active in the women's parallel civic and philanthropic structure would also become active in the WHPA, which brought political pressure on city government for a variety of issues. Five of the twelve chairwomen assigned to wards later became officers and members of the WHPA.

In the months after the closing of the relief stations, families worked hard to rebuild their homes and to bring order out of the tragedy of their lives. But five months after the disaster, women who had been members of the city's social and philanthropic leadership were ready to invest again in the city's future. In February 1901 Isabella Kopperl, a member of the Board of Lady Managers for the Galveston Orphans' Home and the Letitia Rosenberg Women's Home, held an open house tea. Among the guests was Anna

Maxwell Jones, who lived in New York but came back to Galveston, her childhood home, every year. At that moment Jones was mounting a campaign for a women's civic association that would transform the city. She spoke not so much about the past as about the future: "You brave people of Galveston have buried the dead, clothed the naked and fed the hungry. Now you must not stop at that. You must safe guard the Beach of the City, plant trees and flowers, and make it again the City Beautiful." Waldine Kopperl, Isabella's daughter-in-law, recorded,

I think Anna [Maxwell Jones] can justly be called the Inspirer and Founder of the Health Protective Association, for its spirit, its aims were hers. . . . When Anna got up everyone clapped. . . . We all caught fire from Anna's inspired talk, and I think each woman silently consecrated herself for further service for Galveston. She was the real Founder for we took fire from her idea. We all had worked so hard and were oh, so fatigued and stunned with the tragedy of it all, and we needed just that heart counsel that Anna so well knew how to give.

On March 3, 1901, the day the relief committee submitted its final report in the Galveston *Daily News*, an announcement appeared heralding the creation of a new organization made up entirely of white women. As one chapter in the history of the island's great crisis closed, another was opening. Two days later, sixty-six women met at the Y.M.C.A. to form the Women's Health Protective Association. They came from the women's church and synagogue societies, the boards of lady managers for the benevolent institutions, literary and musical clubs, patriotic-hereditary societies, and the Red Cross. Among the members of the first executive committee were: Magnolia Sealy, wife of the city's prominent banker George Sealy, who had entertained Clara Barton and her entourage in their home; Lucy Ballinger Mills, daughter of Judge William Pitt Ballinger and Hallie Ballinger, founder of the Galveston Orphans' Home; and Isabella Kopperl, philanthropist and niece of the founder of Temple B'nai Israel. Although the founders represented old-guard Galveston, the

WHPA quickly became an organization for the middle classes and a younger generation that brought the city into the twentieth century. The initiators announced in the *Daily News* that "the time had come when the Galveston women rich and poor, club women and non-club women, must work hand in hand and heart to heart to make Galveston a beautiful town and a law abiding place, and the only way to do this is to have the cooperation of every woman in the city. . . ."

The WHPA's direction toward greater democracy among white women distinguished it from women's clubs of the previous century. Those had been private, exclusive, and self-perpetuating; the WHPA was open to all adult white women; they elected their own officers—ten executive officers as well as seventeen or more standing committee chairwomen and ad hoc committee chairwomen. At first the elected leadership represented old established Galveston families, but later the offices went to women who worked hard and were competent and energetic regardless of class. By 1916, the WHPA had succeeded where no other women's club had before; its membership totaled five hundred and it had become one of the strongest political pressure groups in the city. Through the WHPA, women gave themselves the authority to investigate city problems and work toward their solutions, even if it meant challenging male leadership at city hall.

The WHPA embodied a political agenda from the very beginning. Thus the members, whether they thought they were formally entering politics or not, found themselves endorsing, petitioning, and lobbying—all political acts. Indeed, one of their first decisions was a political one. "To inspire the women of Galveston to a realization of their municipal obligations," they determined to support the bill to adopt the city commission plan for a new city government. Mary Landes, first WHPA president, and whose husband Henry would become mayor in 1905, headed a subcommittee to draw up a resolution to form "City Commission Government." Hundreds of women signed the resolution and sent it to the state legislature in Austin. Then as nonvoting citizens they let it be known that they expected the men "to vote . . . for those men who will help to rehabilitate and restore the town to a place not hitherto attained."

The first priority for the WHPA was sanitation. Its very name indicates its initial purpose. No doubt the title was familiar to those just entering the Progressive Era, the years between 1895 and 1925, when the nation underwent an extensive period of reform, especially in towns and cities. Reformers were often middle-class men and women who were aware that runaway unregulated capitalism and industrialization had created problems for the nation's workers and for urban centers that remained in industrial zones. Women in New York had created a Ladies Health Protective Association to fight dirty slaughterhouses and garbage scows; in Philadelphia a Woman's Health Protective Association found the water nearly contaminated and demanded a new water filter system. These were among the forty organizations that banded together to form an umbrella group, Health Protective Associations.

The Galveston Women's Health Protective Association concerned itself first with problems created by the storm, which had brought horrific social disorder—thousands of dead buried or cremated, loss of vegetation, destruction of homes and businesses, filth and slime deposited by the high water—not to mention people's carelessness in disposing of their own refuse. The WHPA took its cue from Dr. George A. Soper, who had instructed the CRC on cleaning and sanitizing the city after the hurricane. Soper had preached to the council members, the mayor, and the city health department on the proper way to sanitize the city, but he had one more word for the women: "the good housewife [should gather] up the refuse for collection by the health wagons." City health and sanitation depended as much on women as on men; in fact it began with the housewife. Progressives called this "municipal housekeeping"—women had as much to do with keeping their city clean as with their own homes. Because, they said, how can one's home be kept clean if the city's bakeries, meat markets, dairies, and water supply were filthy?

With this concept, the model of the Red Cross, the inspiration

of Anna Maxwell Jones, and with the determination to participate in the city's resurrection, Galveston women discovered new power within their ranks. They finally mobilized for action and drew up a constitution with an agenda:

to promote the health of the people of Galveston and the cleanliness of the city by taking such action from time to time as may secure the enforcement of the existing sanitary laws and regulations by calling the attention of the proper authorities to any violation thereof, and to procure the amendment of such laws and regulations when they shall be found inefficient for the prevention of acts injurious to the public health or the cleanliness of the city; and to promote the beauty of the city of Galveston by encouraging the planting of trees, shrubbery, flowers and otherwise.

More specifically WHPA members created committees to inspect the sanitary condition of jails, schools, stables, streetcars, markets (corner groceries and fruit stands), streets and alleys, cemeteries, dairies, fountains, esplanades, public parks and monuments, and beaches. The presence of a police matron for women in the city and county jails also caught their attention. To keep members informed they printed in their bylaws the city codes and ordinances. No city laws existed for regulating areas of public health that women found crucial—public schools, jails, cemeteries, or dairies. Families still used privies and outhouses because the city did not require houses to be connected to the sewerage system. City council did have a law against spitting, a practice that many believed spread tuberculosis, yet the women learned that the police did not enforce it! WHPA members felt as if male leaders had abandoned their duties to the citizens of Galveston. The mayor and city council were simply acting under older notions of the limits of government where the cardinal rule was not to interfere with private enterprise. Regulation was a progressive idea espoused by a new generation of activists. It would take time before government responded to the new ideas for responsive, proactive government.

Publicizing an absence of city regulation over areas of public health played right into the hands of commission government advocates. When the WHPA reported on the condition of jails, stables, alleys, streets, and markets, the public became aware of the need for stricter sanitation rulings. Now voters had another reason—besides fiscal responsibility—to support governmental reform. Subtly, the WHPA influenced public opinion in the matter of municipal reform.

In the twelve months following the hurricane, in addition to reporting on sanitation, women chose to concentrate on reburial of storm victims. Estimates of the dead ran as high as 3,000 corpses found in the rubble, 1,000 discovered on streets and in yards, 500 drowned in the Gulf of Mexico, and another 500 swept to the north. Possibly another thousand died on the mainland. For months and years later—as late as 1908—skeletons were still being found. The WHPA assumed responsibility for bodies that had been hastily buried in the sand or in yards and for those that continued to appear. Once the Central Relief Committee disbanded, the WHPA took over disposal of the dead, and Galveston citizens went to this organization for reburial of storm victims rather than to city hall. In this way, the WHPA become a service arm of city government. Members transported remains to the cemetery at the west end of the island and voted "to take charge of the little cemetery of the unknown dead," wherein they raised a granite headstone to mark the graves. The organization was fortunate to have allies in the New York State Federation of Women's Clubs, which, through the urging of Anna Maxwell Jones, sent $1,000 for reburial expenses, and in Governor Sayers, who sent $1,148 for the "reinterment of storm victims not properly buried."

The sensibilities of all citizens, but especially of these ladies, were shocked by the way in which the dead were so unceremoniously discarded, burned, or cast into the sea. Even though grief had gripped the community at the time, the primary concern had been protection of the living. So there had been few proper funeral services. It seemed fitting, then, for the WHPA, which had assumed responsibility for the city's grave tending, to hold a memorial service on the first anniversary of the hurricane.

The Lucas Terrace apartments, in which over fifty people died (and twenty-two survived), symbolized the curse—as well as the hope—stemming from the storm. There, on scaffolding perched atop the rubble and in the midst of a sea of flowers sent by relatives and friends, seven thousand people attended a service on September 8, 1901, to commemorate the dead and give hope to the living. Attendees paid tribute, heard the sad eulogies, and remembered the terror of that night. But once again, faith in the future stole the show. Already plans were under way to build a protective sea wall and to raise the city. "Out of the darkness of desolation and death the glorious sunshine of hope arises, and we have basked in its rays today. . . . We should build stronger and on higher ground. Elevate the Gulf front of the city, and construct a breakwater similar to our jetties. . . ." Grateful citizens thanked the WHPA—"these noble women [who] joined themselves together under the name of the Women's Health Protective Association." The ceremony concluded by sending the children—the island's hope for the future—off to plant sprigs of oleanders and salt cedars in the sand.

As the members of the CRC said their farewells, closed their offices, and gave their final reports, they looked back on incredible accomplishments: $1,258,000 collected for relief and rebuilding, streets cleared, bodies disposed of, commercial structures rebuilt, homes once again occupied, citizens gainfully employed, banks opened, and hope reborn. The Strand resumed its commercial position, and the wharves were alive with ships. Only the mayor and twelve aldermen waited unhappily for their dismissal by the voters. On September 18, 1901, the city opened its doors under new management.

CHAPTER THREE

"Everything that mortal men can do"

Protecting Galveston Island

The Grade Raising Board is doing everything that mortal men

can do to succeed in their stupendous undertaking, and we

believe that success is assured.

E. R. CHEESBOROUGH TO W. H. PLUMMER, JANUARY 1904

DEALING WITH GALVESTON's most pressing needs immediately after the storm kept everyone busy for months, but as the cleanup and recovery progressed, city leaders were forced to consider the long-term effects of the storm and how best to regain the island's premier economic position within the state and region. Houston leaders, always ready to capitalize on Galveston's misfortune, cautioned investors away from the island city, and the devastation seemed to reinforce the point. Such a precarious physical location, the destruction of tax base and infrastructure, the massive loss of life and subsequent departure of thousands of residents—surely, Galveston was headed the way of Indianola, a once thriving coastal town wiped out by a hurricane's wrath in 1886. But there was still a deep water channel, largely intact piers, a committed business community, and a population resolved to live on an unprotected sandbar.

Almost immediately after the storm, citizens vowed to return and rebuild. "It is not time yet to talk of the future," commented the Galveston *Tribune* four days later, "except to say it is all ours, and when we are fed, clothed and healed we shall seize it all and make it glorious. . . ." In reply to an inquiry from "a great New York paper" as to whether the community would rebuild, the Galveston *Daily News* answered "that Galveston did not intend to succumb to her crushing misfortune, but would again resume her place as the great port of the gulf. . . ." Optimistic but wary of future occurrences, the *Engineering Record* gravely counseled that "before the city can assume the importance its geographical position renders possible, it must be made safe against such inundations as wrecked it a fortnight ago. . . ."

What may be surprising is the absence of discussion about abandoning the island. Days after the storm, W. L. Moody Sr. told an interviewer

Galveston will be rebuilt stronger and better than ever before. It is necessary to have a city here. Even if the storm had swept the island bare of every human habitation and every structure and left it as barren as it was before civilized man set foot on the place, still men would come here and build a city because a port is demanded at this place.

Southern Pacific railroad, a crucial corporate presence in the port and on the island, had invested $1 million constructing facilities at the port in 1899 and wasted no time in announcing the order of a new two-track bridge to cross the bay. Perhaps most significant, if Galveston did not rebuild, many wealthy individuals stood to lose millions of dollars that were already invested in island enterprises. As relief efforts were scaled down, and some kind of normalcy returned to the town, thoughts turned to the future and how to make it bright.

Central Relief Committee (CRC) member Isaac H. ("Ike") Kempner considered what would be necessary for Galveston's business resurgence. This was something of a tricky issue. The idea of building a sea wall was attractive—but if the island was really a safe place, if the storm was a tragic anomaly and/or random event, then building a sea wall or taking other precautionary measures seemed to acknowledge the city's precarious position. On the other hand, without some moves by Galveston leaders to calm fears of future calamity, people would not return, rebuild, and invest. Clearly, any actions taken had to be publicly framed very carefully. Galveston would take steps to protect itself, leaders agreed, because the city was too important *not* to rebuild in the best manner possible. And, in order to pacify and appease those who felt anxious about future storms, precautionary measures would be implemented—just in

case, many years down the line, another hurricane might threaten. Where, then, to begin?

As a member of the finance committee, Kempner knew firsthand the state of the city's coffers. Somewhat troubled before the storm, municipal finances were appalling in the aftermath. Besides pre-storm indebtedness, the city carried a staggering load of relief debt and faced the ongoing responsibility for repairing or replacing city services and equipment. In addition, some steps had to be taken to guarantee that such overwhelming damage would never recur; the island had to protect itself from future hurricanes. From 1901 until 1904, Kempner and other Galveston leaders worked to develop plans that addressed all of these issues. Their solution— a radical change in government and two amazing civil engineering projects—brought Galveston back as an economic player in the region and inspired confidence in both residents and investors.

Probably no municipal government could have met the demands of so vast and complete a disaster, but Galveston political leaders were more ill-equipped than most. The city was governed by a traditional mayor/council system with twelve aldermen elected by wards, but some local residents, inspired by national Progressive reform efforts, had been trying since the early 1890s to combat what they saw as the corrupt, self-interested, unbusinesslike administration of city operations. Amendments passed in 1890 kept the twelve ward-based representatives but added four aldermen elected at large from the entire city. Reformers pushed for even more at-large representation, and a compromise plan developed in 1895 reduced the number of aldermen to twelve but specified that all of them would be elected at large. Each candidate still had to reside within the ward that he represented. This compromise effectively eliminated black representation in city government since the historically black ward no longer selected its alderman based on ward votes alone, and no black candidate could expect to win a citywide election. Norris Wright Cuney, prominent black Republican, businessman, and former alderman, supported reform efforts but voted against the proposal for totally at-large elections.

Political and economic leadership circles in the city only rarely overlapped. Elective office carried little prestige and paid poorly. Honest men could make a better living any number of other ways, and there was little incentive for middle- or upper-class citizens to dirty themselves in the day-to-day brawling of Galveston city politics. Because Galveston's working class was so inextricably tied to the port, union members could usually be convinced that their interests more often than not coincided with plans of the city's white elite. Real political power lay with a committee unique to Galveston and focused on economic development of the island port.

When engineer James B. Eads proved that properly designed jetties could result in the scouring, or deepening, of a channel, Galveston leaders formed a "Committee on Deep Water" in 1881, later known as the Deep Water Committee (DWC), to meet with Eads and explore the possibility of building such jetties for Galveston. After meeting with the engineer and being convinced that such a scheme would work, the committee began serious lobbying efforts at all levels of government to gain funding for the deepening of Galveston channel. This effort ended successfully when Galveston was selected by the federal government as the primary port for the western Gulf of Mexico, and Washington appropriated the necessary funds for jetty construction. Membership on the DWC was confined to a wealthy and powerful elite; most participants were bank and corporate leaders and some served on the Galveston Wharf Company board of directors as well.

Once they had secured their goal of a deep water channel for Galveston, the committee did not disband. The members took to heart their reason for being—the economic health of the city—and simply moved on to other issues that they believed affected the island business climate. And, they came to think, there were serious concerns to be addressed at city hall. Quietly, and always from behind the scenes, the committee began to formulate suggestions for reform even before the storm, and the largest newspapers, controlled for the most part by committee members, printed editorials that hinted broadly at corruption, mismanagement, and the need for a new city charter. The local chamber of commerce and other business interests supported the committee's work and waited for an opportunity to push for broad changes.

Galveston's strong labor presence was reflected in the city's politics. In 1895 two longshoremen, a saloon keeper, a bartender, a drayman, a journeyman printer, a small grocer, a butcher, a real estate salesman, a railroad promoter, and a black politician sat on the city council—hardly candidates from any area boardrooms. That same year, a new organization, the Galveston Good Government Club, was formed to solicit candidates more attuned (or so they stated) to the island's ultimate commercial interests. The club had difficulty recruiting the middle-class businessmen and professionals that it wanted, and the race quickly devolved into a "People" versus "Interests" election, especially when a "People's Ticket" ran for office against the "Good Government" slate. The Good Government Club tried to avoid class issues, claiming that its goal was the businesslike administration of city government. Their argument struck a chord with the voters, and the club ticket successfully elected the mayor, Ashley W. Fly, and eight of the twelve alderman positions. Little changed in 1897, when the Good Government slate became the "Citizens Club" and won all contests. By 1898, however, labor interests had regrouped. Fly had supported action against black dock workers who had struck the Mallory Company, which further damaged his position with working-class voters. In response to the Citizens Club, a "Greater Galveston" ticket composed of candidates purporting to represent common, working-class Galvestonians entered the municipal contest. Walter C. Jones, the city's police chief, was elected mayor, and the Greater Galveston slate won six of the twelve alderman positions. This unfortunately created a council that frequently deadlocked, supporting the perception that city government was ineffectual. The election of aldermen committed to efficient administration and reform did not result in any marked improvement in city operations, nor did the apparent sharing of power that came out of the 1899 election.

City streets were in widespread disrepair, sanitary conditions were abominable, the council did not meet its September 1899 payroll until December, and charges of favoritism and mismanagement plagued the council. Constant deficits required the regular floating of bonds to cover the shortfall, and nothing indicated that the situation was likely to improve. Even before the storm, Alderman C. H. McMaster requested that the council obtain copies of other city charters from around the country so that the group could explore ways to ameliorate the city's plight. Repair of the system would not go far enough, thought many; radical action was in order. Members of the DWC and other local business interests strongly supported efforts to alter the political landscape.

After the storm, infrastructure and services were nonexistent, and only the most extreme exertions recovered water, power, and communication capabilities. When Mayor Walter C. Jones named so many members of the Deep Water Committee to positions on the Central Relief Committee, it seemed an admission that city government was not up to the task at hand. With almost half of the city's taxable property destroyed, upward of two hundred thousand dollars of floating debt—not to mention the expense of repairing city property—drastic measures seemed even more essential, at least to the DWC.

In November 1900, members of the DWC began meeting on a regular basis to draw up a new city charter proposal. Three lawyers were responsible for the first draft: Walter B. Gresham, a former congressman; R. Waverly Smith, a bank president and former president of the Good Government Club; and Farrell D. Minor, a well-known local attorney. The three men and those they consulted looked toward appointed commissions as a viable alternative. The commissions that governed Memphis, Tennessee (during a yellow fever epidemic in 1878), and Washington, D.C., were instructive examples of what might be achieved. Most of all, the men wanted a body that would organize and operate city government like a business, imposing regulation and administration to fulfill municipal responsibilities and provide necessary services. Their condemnation of the existing system was scathing:

Certainly no set of public officials ever seemed so indifferent to the welfare, safety, and health as the ruling majority of those now in office.

. . . Businessmen and methods are what we need now in Galveston, men who know their duty to the city and are not afraid to perform it.

Changing the government was "a question with us of civic life or death." Their plan called for the appointment of five city commissioners by the governor, each one charged with administering a single department: finance and revenue, police and fire, waterworks and sewerage, streets and public improvements. The entire commission, sitting as a body, would make policy decisions.

Once the plan was formulated, the DWC moved to have it passed by the state legislature, since Texas had no provision for home rule. New city charters had to be approved by the legislature, and the DWC worked to obtain the broadest possible base of support, lobbying locally as well as statewide for passage. DWC members controlled both local newspapers, so there was little opposition to the proposal in print, but a few citizens read the proposal and thought through its implications. As written, the commission plan called for the appointment of all five members by the governor, virtually banishing democratic government from the island. Supporters claimed that provisions for electing commission members would be implemented after recovery from the storm was complete, but this seemed disingenuous to some. The sitting city council eventually developed its own proposal for a new city charter that left the system largely intact. Both bills were introduced in the legislature by Galveston Representative Thomas H. Nolan.

Both sides tried to show broad support for their respective plans. The city council focused on the elimination of elections that the DWC plan entailed, while the DWC staked its claim on efficient, businesslike management. The DWC lobbied a convention of the Fort Worth Board of Trade, suggesting that the fate of Galveston and its port was a determining factor in the economic health of the entire state. Island residents appeared to be quite willing to give up their right to elect their leaders, and the DWC commission plan received surprisingly widespread backing from most Galvestonians. The efficiency and integrity of the CRC suggested that a city government run by the same people would be equally effective and successful. Historians Bradley R. Rice and Stephen P. Kretzmann point to four reasons the commission plan was so easily accepted. First, many believed that only a radical and complete change in government would provide the organization and stability necessary to obtain funding for rebuilding, refinancing debt, and constructing protective measures against future hurricanes. Second, most believed that the commission would eventually be elected, that a completely governor-appointed body was only temporary. Third, given the extent of the disaster and the road that the city faced to recovery, most people simply trusted the judgment of the DWC and its adherents. And finally, members of the working-class believed their interests would be protected. Hadn't Mayor Jones been elected in part through labor votes?

As chairman of the CRC, Jones was seen by labor leaders as their representative on that body. Union members participated extensively in the cleanup, with Screwmen's Benevolent Association members serving as security forces before the militia arrived. As the recovery progressed and housing became a pressing issue, William V. McConn had been named to the building committee. Editor of the working-class Galveston *Journal*, McConn and his newspaper spoke for organized labor in the city. His appointment reflected the CRC's commitment to consensus and to courting labor support for upcoming changes in the political structure. McConn convinced the other members of the building committee that union labor should be used to construct the bulk of the commissary houses. The Deep Water Committee and its proxy, the CRC, cultivated Jones and McConn. As the commission issue was being debated in Austin, McConn discouraged Galveston labor leaders from proposing their own commissioner candidates and counseled the locals to stay out of politics. Organized labor, especially the white construction trades, benefited greatly from the building projects and recovery efforts funded and administered by the CRC. McConn and others were convinced that labor interests would be protected.

The opponents of the bill recognize that organized labor has been a potent force in securing the unanimity of the people of Galveston in support of the measure and that in the nature of things such organized labor will be accorded a representative on the board when appointed.

McConn was to be disappointed; the first five commissioners had no ties to organized labor. Union support of the move to commission government—no matter how antidemocratic—is still understandable in this context. As historian Kretzmann points out,

Jobs and profits depended on restoring the shipping industry's confidence in the safety of the port and the competence of the city's government. Some Galveston workers understood that the commission charter would probably cost them influence [in] city politics, but opposition to the plan might cost them their jobs.

Some non-Galveston lawmakers, however, were deeply troubled by the abandonment of democratic principles and sided with the opposition. Threatened with failure and strongly committed to the passage of the plan, commission backers and legislators negotiated an amendment that made the proposal acceptable. Two of the commissioners would be elected at large, thus providing at least an appearance of popular participation without endangering the appointed majority. The bill granting a new city charter to Galveston became law on July 7, 1901, and the new city commission took office on September 18 of that year. Judge William T. Austin, one of the elected commissioners, was named mayor-president, and the other elected commissioner, A. P. Norman, a livestock dealer, was placed in charge of police and fire. The governor appointed three other commissioners: Isaac H. Kempner, finance and revenue; Herman C. Lange, waterworks and sewerage; and Valery Austin, streets and public improvements.

Was there truly a need for a completely new form of city government? Historians examining the issue differ in their responses. Mayors and council members prior to the commission were not of the same class as members of the DWC or most of the other business leaders of the community, nor did they possess near the financial clout. Critics of the DWC and their ostensible reform efforts charge that Galveston's city government was no worse than that of any other nineteenth-century urban center, but there were ongoing financial problems that hampered city operations. An audit in 1895 revealed that no trial balance had been taken since 1891, and the official accountant knew no bookkeeping. The issuing of bonds to cover unfunded debt rankled businessmen, and poor services were a continual annoyance. No doubt the Progressive movement heightened awareness of both problems and potential solutions, but, more than that, the destruction caused by the September hurricane pushed the issue. If Galveston was to recover for the long term, to regain its commercial prominence, the city had to prove that it could solicit, obtain, and administer millions of dollars in a responsible way. Through the commission form of government, Galveston got its municipal house in order before entertaining prospective financial suitors, even as it placed power in the hands of a wealthy elite and curtailed popular participation in electoral politics.

Once installed, the new commission moved rapidly to develop long-term plans for the island's safety. On September 25, 1901, a resolution was passed to appoint a committee charged with selecting competent engineers to report on protection plans for the city. On November 20, based on recommendations from the committee, the city commission appointed a board of engineers composed of General H. M. Robert, Alfred Noble, and H. C. Ripley to plan protective measures for Galveston. The engineers were instructed to develop

plans and specifications with estimates of the cost: First, for the safest and most efficient ways of protecting said City against overflows from the Sea. Second: for elevating, filling, and grading the avenues, streets, side-walks, alleys and lots of said City . . . and to secure sufficient elevation for drainage and sewerage [and] Third, for a breakwater or seawall of sufficient strength and height to prevent the overflow of and damage to said City from the Gulf.

During storms, the island faced flooding from both the Gulf of Mexico to the southeast and its channel to Galveston Bay on the northwest. Any protective measures had to address rising water on either side of the narrow landmass.

At a public meeting on January 25, 1902, the engineers submitted their report. In it, they described original grading surveys initiated in 1875, outlined conditions under which the island regularly flooded, and offered anecdotal evidence as to the heights of each of these floods. The 1875 grading survey fixed the elevation of Broadway at 8 feet, a level that was later raised to 9, with the grade descending from that point toward the Gulf and the bay. Nowhere was the island higher than 8.9 feet, and the average elevation from 6th Street to 39th Street was 5.8 feet. West of 39th Street the elevation declined to an average of 3.7 feet. The first flood in recorded memory occurred in 1834; elderly Galvestonians recalled that the island had been completely submerged. The engineers went on to list six other inundations that had resulted in floodwaters up to 9.5 feet in some places. But the worst by far had been the storm of the previous year, when "the water reached a height exceeding by far any previous records at Galveston." The deepest flooding had been at Shulte's store, located at 8th Street and Avenue B (The Strand), where the water measured 15.7 feet, but depths of 10 to 14 feet were recorded at twelve other locations. More than high water, the engineers also noted that

The direction of currents at different stages of the overflow varied greatly throughout the city. . . . the water came upon the island first at the east end and south side, but before the water had gone entirely across the island it was met by water from the bay at a point relatively near the bay side, and the waters uniting rushed to the west.

They went on to recount that "the greatest destruction was caused by currents and wave action." It was this wave action, in conjunction with the absolute increase in water volume, that was responsible for the horrendous destruction visited upon the island in 1900. The engineers concluded that

[p]rotection from storms is not only required for the preservation of life

and property, but also . . . to give confidence to the people of Galveston and to others who may be drawn here by business interests, in the absolute safety of the city against the recurrence of such catastrophes as the one of 1900. The Board is of the opinion that it is practicable, at an expense not large, compared with the results obtained, to place Galveston entirely out of reach of any storm like those from which she suffered previous to 1900 . . . and at the same time make the city safe from any serious damage from water in a storm like the one of 1900.

The report continued,

To accomplish these objects the Board would propose . . . the building of a solid concrete wall, over three miles long, . . . the top of this wall to be 17 feet above mean lowwater, or 1.3 feet higher than the highest point reached by the water in the storm of 1900. Second: The raising of the city grade . . . Third: The making of an embankment on top of this fill adjacent to the wall . . .

The engineers proposed a system whose three components would work together to prevent wave and water damage associated with the periodic hurricanes that ravaged the city. The raising of the city grade was necessary to get the streets and lots sufficiently high for safety to life and property "in severe storms. The seawall was necessary to protect the filling from the force of the waves." They went on to stress the importance of the filling. "The filling proposed is to be made over the city, together with the embankment immediately behind the seawall, is hardly less indispensable than the seawall itself. It places the entire city area above the height of ordinary floods."

In matters of expense, the three advisors calculated unit prices and total costs. The sea wall was determined to cost $66.50 a linear foot. With engineering fees and contingencies added, Galveston could have its bulwark for $1,294,755. The grade raising, the second component of the master plan, was determined to require 13,873,000 cubic yards of fill costing $.10 a yard. After adding expenses of paving and soil placement at $7.40 a linear foot, pro-

jected costs for raising large sections of the island were $2,210,285. "Total cost of entire project recommended by the Board, $3,505,040, or say, $3,500,000."

Galveston residents were more than willing to accept the advice and recommendations of these engineers. Besides possessing a genuine desire to rebuild their city, islanders had great faith in the expertise of the committee called upon to solve their problems. Robert, Ripley, and Noble were prominent members of a growing class of urban planning professionals. Robert and Ripley were both retired from the U.S. Army Corps of Engineers, had visited or served many years in Galveston, and had worked throughout the Galveston District. Alfred Noble was an engineer as well, had been involved with the construction of Chicago's breakwater, and was then serving as president of the American Society of Civil Engineers. Such experts in technology held great status within the Progressive movement as holders of highly specialized knowledge whose employment could lead to the creation of safer, healthier, and more beautiful urban environments. They were believed to be above petty politics and focused upon making cities less hostile to their inhabitants. And the engineers maintained faith in their own expertise as well, as evidenced by an *Engineering News* editorial, which opined, "if the city desires to save itself from a repetition of the recent calamity, it is quite within the resources of engineering to furnish the desired protection."

Public and private support for the proposal was quickly forthcoming. Financing was another question. The new city commissioners had allowed the city to default on $17,500 worth of forty-year bonds issued in 1881. Negotiations with bondholders resulted in the lowering of interest rates on remaining outstanding issues. But given the decimation of the tax base, the existing bonded indebtedness, a new and untried government, and the size of the bond issue required, Galveston could not issue bonds to cover sea wall and grade raising construction. Contemporary accounts of this period make no mention of the city's bond indebtedness problem but claim overriding community support for underwriting the costs. Using as evidence the amount of taxes paid to the county by residents of Galveston, city and county commissioners reached an agreement whereby the county would issue bonds for sea wall construction and the city would finance the grade raising. Before the bonds for sea wall construction could be issued, however, consent of two thirds of the taxpayers of the entire county was necessary. By the time the county's request for a $1.5 million issue came to a vote, 84 percent of the bonds' purchase price had been pledged. With a 98 percent turnout, the bond issue authorization passed 3,119 to 22. The newspaper noted "A Grand Jollification" in response to the vote. In addition, the twenty-seventh Texas State Legislature donated, for grade raising purposes, two-years' worth of the city's ad valorem taxes and a portion of the occupation and poll taxes. The following session of the legislature extended the period of donation to fifteen years.

The idea of building a sea wall to protect portions of Galveston island was not new. All kinds of barricades—dikes, levees, or berms—were standard engineering methods used to protect vulnerable shorelines and riverbanks. Damage caused by a severe hurricane in 1875 prompted discussions of building such a structure, but Galvestonians were unwilling to pay for the project themselves and unable to convince the state legislature to fund the work in the interests of regional commerce. In 1878 salt cedar trees were planted along the old dune line in an effort to accumulate sand and to form a natural barrier to waves and rising water. After another storm in 1886 destroyed the gulf community of Indianola, a group of thirty businessmen formed the Progressive Association and issued a public resolution calling for the construction of a sea wall. This group lobbied the state legislature and secured passage of an amendment to the city charter that authorized issuance of bonds to fund protective works. In addition, the group contacted James B. Eads, an engineer famous for improvements to the mouth of the Mississippi, who submitted a plan for a twelve-foot embankment. A bond issue met with fierce resistance, and the island lapsed into a false sense of security as the years passed with no storm-driven damage. On September 1, 1900, with eerie prescience, Colonel H. M. Robert, then divisional engineer of the

U.S. Army, presented to Galveston City Council a plan for the "improvement, protection, and development of Galveston Harbor" that included construction of a dike "that would form a wall diverting the heavy storm tides from the northeast and thus protect Galveston from overflow." On September 16, 1900—only eight days after the storm—David Hall, "one of the creditors of the city," wrote the *Daily News* to advocate the building of a sea wall. Supporters were not without other suggestions. By September 28, 1900, the New York *Herald* had published ideas for Galveston's safety that included building a sea wall, having a "day-time Galveston" (for business) on the present site and a "night-time Galveston" (for sleeping) on the mainland, rebuilding the city on steel or wooden piles as a "modern Venice," consolidating with Houston, or completely removing the city to Port Arthur, Sabine Pass, or Aransas. One of the most creative suggestions came from France, where a colonel in the artillery advocated "a plan to erect a battery for destroying hurricanes close to Galveston. . . . If a West Indian cyclone approached he would fire at it and . . . break its back."

With financing secured, Galveston County proceeded with plans and construction of the first segment of the sea wall. Technology for such building was well known and work progressed quickly. Specifications for the sea wall were published in June of 1902, the construction contract was let to J. M. O'Rourke and Company in September, and the first pile was driven on October 28, 1902. Supporters of organized labor pressed for union workers in the project, and the Galveston *Journal* noted that labor support of the city commission had helped gain approval of the project. Besides, as evidenced by the construction of the commissary houses, union workers did good work at good prices. In the end, union workers were utilized where possible, but there was little call for skilled labor in sea wall construction.

In their report the three engineers described the project as

a solid concrete wall, over 3 miles long, connecting with the south jetty near Eighth Street; thence to Sixth and D; thence across the island and down the beach as far as Thirty-ninth Street. The top of this wall to be

17 feet above mean low water, or 1.3 feet higher than the highest point reached by the water in the storm of 1900.

The Gulf face of the wall was curved so that waves would be forced upward and the structure's foundation was to be piles that would be protected from undermining by sheet piling and riprap. At the bottom, the wall would be sixteen feet wide, at the top, five feet.

Specifications described in great detail the process for building the wall. It was to be constructed in fifty-foot lengths, in alternating sections, using forms to mold the concrete.

Trenches for the piles were specified in addition to the exact order of construction. Piles for each section were to be of long- or short-leaf pine, and "[t]hey shall not vary more than six (6) inches from a straight line connecting the ends." The timber was to be "free of decay and unsound or large knots. The diameter of the small end shall not be less than ten (10) inches, and they shall be thirty (30) feet in length, unless shorter piles are authorized in writing by the engineer." The pilings, spaced on four-foot centers, were to be driven into the sand until 2.5 feet remained above ground, at which point the bark was to be cleaned from the surface so that the pile would imbed cleanly into the concrete.

A continuous line of what was called Wakefield sheet piling was to be driven in such a way as to prevent water from seeping under the wall. Once the pilings had been set, forms for the wall were positioned and the section built "rapidly and continuously, each layer being placed before the preceding layer has fully set, to prevent the formation of horizontal joints." The concrete was to be made of 380 pounds of "slow setting Portland cement," to 9 cubic feet of sand and 22.5 cubic feet of broken stone. Once the concrete was poured into the forms, the contractor was enjoined from removing the forms any less than three days after completing the section and not even then if the concrete had not hardened sufficiently. Once the wall itself had been formed, riprap—sandstone boulders varying from two hundred to one thousand pounds—was to be placed three feet deep and twenty-seven feet outward from the "sea face" to protect the wall's foundation. The riprap was to be deposited so that

the larger pieces were on top, with smaller stones filling the "interstices." The object was to present a surface to oncoming waves that was as smooth as possible without the meticulous placement of each rock.

In reply to questions from W. Watson Davis at Alabama Polytechnic Institute, E. R. Cheesborough described the process of filling the forms:

the sand which had accumulated over the top of the piling previously driven for the foundation was removed so that the earth would be removed down to the waterline, or what is known as mean low tide. The mixing machine, which is constructed so as to run on two railroad tracks, straddeling [sic] the excavation . . . moves along depositing each batch of mixed concrete. There are men down in the excavation with heavy iron tampers who tamp the material. A distance of 100 feet is covered. The mixing machine is rolled back to the beginning point and a second layer put in. Wooden pieces are then placed on top of mixed concrete thus put in so as to form a lock and then the molds formed by these wooden pieces running along the top of the foundation are filled. The foundation is then completed.

The contractor built the wall for the most part according to the committee's specifications, except that the embankment was narrowed to 100 feet with a maximum elevation of 16.6 feet—changes approved by the supervising engineer. After the first piling was driven in October 1902, this earliest sea wall segment was completed in 1904 and ran along the Gulf side of the island for 17,593 feet. While Galveston County was building the sea wall, the federal government authorized construction and extension of the wall across the front of the Fort Crockett military installation, which went from 39th Street to 53rd Street. This added 4,935 more feet to the island's bulwark and connected three gun emplacements. Construction of the federal footage began in December 1904, finished in November 1905, and cost taxpayers $295,000.

The sea wall has been extended several times since this initial effort. The first extension, completed in 1921, was to the east, a

FIGURE 3.1: Once approved by voters, sea wall construction proceeded quickly. Here the mixing machine described by Cheesborough appears to be positioned between two forms for wall sections. (Courtesy Bain Collection, Prints and Photographs Division, Library of Congress, Washington, D.C.)

FIGURE 3.2: In addition to the sea wall protecting the city, the federal government agreed to extend the wall in front of Fort Crockett installation, from 39th Street to 53rd Street. This image, dated March 3, 1905, shows the ongoing march of wall sections on the southeastern face of the island. ("No. 78, Sea wall, April 1905," Folder 062, Fort Crockett, 1902–1906, RG 077, National Archives Southwest Region, Fort Worth, Texas.)

FIGURE 3.3: Looking eastward from Fort Crockett. Note the wide beach in front of the wall; erosion caused by the sea wall continues to wear away island beaches. The city eventually constructed rock groins and adopted a program of "beach renourishment" in an attempt to have the protection afforded by the sea wall and tourist-attracting beaches. ("No. 84, Sea wall, Looking from 2–10 in Batty, Fort Crockett, May 6, 1905," Folder 062, Fort Crockett, 1902–1906, RG 077, National Archives Southwest Region, Fort Worth, Texas.)

FIGURE 3.4: The wall was built in alternating sections, with a tongue-and-groove-like attachment on the sides. The contractor had to let each section dry a minimum of three days. ("No. 71, Sea wall, March 9, 1905," Folder 062, Fort Crockett, 1902–1906, RG 077, National Archives Southwest Region, Fort Worth, Texas.)

FIGURE 3.5: The original sea wall, a combined effort by the city of Galveston and the federal government, ended on the western side of Fort Crockett. The riprap wrapped around the end of the structure in order to prevent gulf waters from undermining and eroding the newly constructed wall. ("No. 12, Sea wall, West end of wall, showing height of riprap. Nov. 3, 1905," Folder 062, Fort Crockett, 1902–1906, RG 077, National Archives Southwest Region, Fort Worth, Texas.)

lengthening of the wall from 6th Street to the first battery at Fort San Jacinto. That segment was extended in 1926 all the way across to the south jetty. Westward expansion soon followed. Galveston County extended the wall from 53rd Street to 61st Street in 1926, a project completed in 1927. The final, three-mile extension of the bulwark was completed in stages from 1951 until 1962. Today the sea wall extends almost ten miles along the Gulf of Mexico side of Galveston Island, protecting nearly one third of the beachfront.

One perhaps unforeseen consequence of the sea wall construction involved erosion of the beach in front of the wall. A hurricane in 1915 washed away most of the sand, and subsequent cycles of tides, winds, and storms did not replenish the area. By 1934 Gulf waters reached the riprap in most places, which threatened the sea wall itself. Engineering studies determined that the erosion process could be stopped and reversed if a system of rock groins was built perpendicular to the wall. Completed in 1936, these groins extend five hundred feet into the Gulf and help to collect and retain sand below water level and somewhat along the beach. In the 1990s Galveston has paid for "beach renourishment," a process by which sand is dredged from nearby Gulf waters and deposited along the shoreline. This procedure is not permanent, however, and must be repeated every few years to keep wide stretches of beach for the tourism industry.

The city's grade raising efforts proceeded along a slightly different path. Successful court challenges to state statutes authorizing the new city commission required the city to provide for the popular election, rather than gubernatorial appointment, of all the city commissioners. Amendments to the city charter also specified that the governor appoint "three resident citizens . . . to constitute a board for the management, control and direction of the work of filling and raising the avenues, streets, sidewalks, alleys, lots and outlots in said city, and to make all expenditures of funds for that purpose." Each expenditure had to be approved by the Board of Commissioners, and each member of the Grade Raising Board— as the board of administrators was called—was required to take an oath of office and provide a five-thousand-dollar bond "for the

FIGURE 3.6: The molds for the wall were filled in layers; a cement-mixing machine moved on a track above the form and poured concrete into the form. Workers below tamped the mixture into place, and the machine retraced its steps in order to deposit another layer. (Courtesy Prints and Photographs Division, Library of Congress, Washington, D.C.)

FIGURE 3.7: Two monuments commemorate the original sea wall dedi-
cation. These large granite posts are
currently located at the foot of 23rd
Street and the sea wall. (Courtesy
Rosenberg Library, Galveston, Texas.)

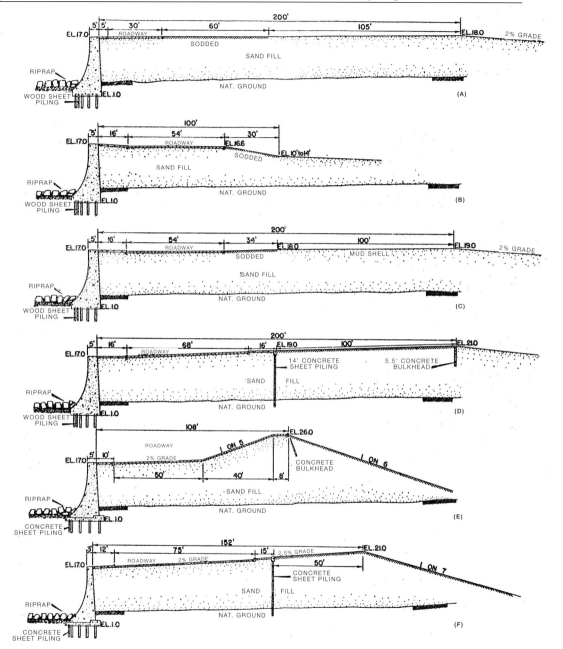

FIGURE 3.8: Six diagrams of the sea wall. (A) the wall proposed by the Robert board; (B) the wall as initially built; (C) the wall as modified after the 1909 hurricane; (D) the wall as modified after the 1915 hurricane; (E) the wall as built to the east, in front of Fort San Jacinto in the 1920s; (F) the wall as authorized for a final three-mile western extension. ("History of the Galveston Seawall," by Albert B. Davis; paper presented at Second Annual Conference on Coastal Engineering, Houston, Texas, November 1951; paper in possession of author.)

faithful performance of his duties." Terms of office were not to exceed two years or extend beyond completion of the work. For their services, members of the board would receive five hundred dollars paid by the city.

On May 15, 1903, Governor Samuel Willis Tucker Lanham announced the appointments of Captain J. P. Alvey, John Sealy, and E. R. Cheesborough. All three men had been active in Galveston business and politics for many years. Alvey was then general manager of the Texas Guarantee and Trust Company and a member of the Texas Land and Loan Company and the school board. John Sealy, scion of a prominent Galveston family, was a member of the banking firm of Hutchings, Sealy and Company, president of the Galveston Wharf Company, and an officer of many other local institutions. E. R. Cheesborough was the youngest of the board of managers but equally well considered. As secretary of the Blum Land Company and secretary-treasurer of the Texas Cement Company, he brought strong administrative talents to the body. Moreover, he had been heavily involved in founding the Galveston Good Government Club, having written to the New York City Good Government organization in 1894 about establishing such a group in the island city. He brought credibility and integrity to the grade raising effort and quickly assumed responsibility for administering the massive project.

Once the Grade Raising Board was in place, events proceeded apace. In June 1903 the board recommended the issuance of $2 million in grade raising bonds and hired a supervising engineer for the project, Captain Charles S. Riché, another former Corps of Engineers Galveston District engineer. A survey of the parts of the island to be filled was begun in July and by September, the board and county and city commissioners agreed to advertise jointly for bids for sixty days and then enter into separate contracts for the filling of the sea wall right-of-way (a county jurisdiction) and the rest of the island (a city purview). Representatives of the county agreed to pay the contractor all cash and the city contracted to pay one third in cash and two thirds in 5 percent grade raising bonds unless the payment of all cash would secure a lower price. Final

specifications for the grade raising were completed September 15, 1903, and bid solicitations were placed in appropriate publications throughout the United States at the beginning of October.

As specified, the bid requested proposals to "raise the grade of the City of Galveston" for four particular areas. Division A was bounded on the north by the south side of Avenue A (now Harborside Drive), on the east and the south by the sea wall right-of-way and on the west by the western side of 13th Street. Division B lay to the southwest of A, confined to the north by the northern side of Broadway, to the east by the western side of 13th Street, to the south by the sea wall right-of-way, and to the west by the eastern side of 32nd Street. Division C moved farther westward, bumping into property controlled by the federal government. It was bordered on the north by the northern line of Broadway, on the east by the eastern side of 32nd Street, on the south by the sea wall right-of-way, and on the west by the "boundary of the general area to be filled as described." The fourth and final area to be filled was the space "from the rear face of the concrete portion of the sea wall towards the city to the boundary of the sea wall right-of-way."

By the 2 P.M. deadline on December 7, 1903, only two bids for the work had been received. Nevertheless, the proposals were opened and after some consultation the contracts were awarded to the firm of Goedhart and Bates of New York on December 12, 1903. The plan outlined by P. C. Goedhart and Lindon Bates was bold. Dredge material would be taken from Galveston Bay by self-loading and discharging self-propelled hopper dredges that would then steam through a distribution canal "to pipe line stations and discharge their loads through pipes running down the streets and avenues." This canal would "parallel the sea wall . . . inside the wall and the city. . . . The earth taken from the canal . . . placed on the sea wall right of way, and when the contract [had] been complied with the dredges [would] back out of the canal, filling it up firmly behind them. . . ." The sea wall right-of-way, controlled by the County Commissioners Court, was to be filled within twelve months from February 18, 1904, and the raising of the city was to be completed by that date in 1907.

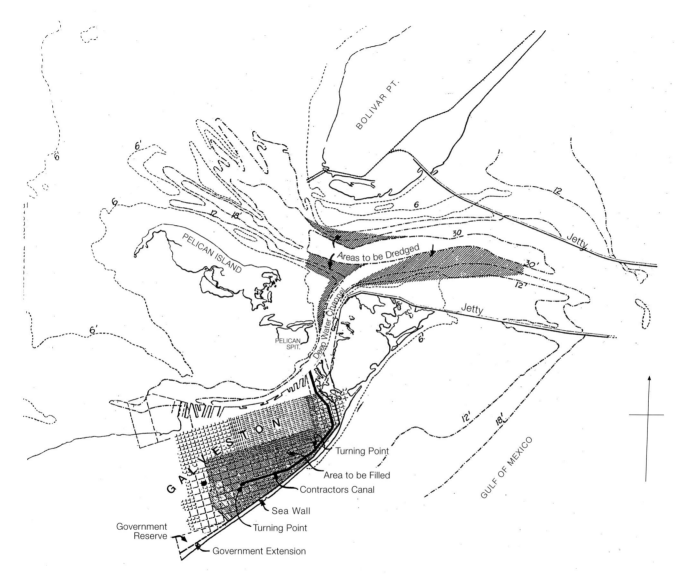

FIGURE 3.9: "Galveston and Vicinity, Showing the Temporary Canal and Area to be Filled." Few areas of Galveston were left undisturbed by the grade raising. Besides being faced with raising their own homes and businesses, some residents confronted a canal through their property. (*Engineering Record*, March 11, 1905.)

The authors of this plan could claim great authority for such work. P. C. Goedhart was the senior member of the Goedhart Brothers engineering firm of Dusseldorf, Germany. That company had worked in the harbors of Dusseldorf, Neuss, Danzig, and Kiel, as well as in the Dortmund-Ems and Amsterdam-Rhine canals. Lindon Bates was the American partner of the firm Goedhart and Bates of New York, inventor of a system of high-powered hydraulic dredges, and had been engaged in the design and implementation of harbor improvements for numerous nations—the United States, Belgium, Egypt, Australia, and India, among others. He had also been involved in the construction of shipping terminals at Kansas City, Missouri; Portland, Oregon; Seattle and Tacoma, Washington; and of the drainage canal at Chicago. Interestingly, the only comparable effort to fill and raise an existing urban area was the grade raising of some parts of Chicago in the mid-nineteenth century.

What appeared to be a reasonably straightforward plan required a monumental administrative effort. Early in the planning process, city leaders had agreed that the city would be responsible for raising streets; trolley lines; gas, water, and sewer pipelines; and whatever other municipal service properties lay in the areas to be raised, as well as for providing the fill for the rest of the process. Private property owners would be responsible for the raising of their improvements—that is, houses, barns, stables, and any other structures located on the blocks to be raised. Excavating a canal so that the dredges could transport fill material necessitated another kind of negotiation with private property owners. The canal route ran parallel to the sea wall and also required a turning basin so that the dredges could discharge their fill and return to Gulf waters to reload. In order to acquire the land for the canal right-of-way, the city agreed to lease the necessary lots from their respective owners, paying as rental fees the taxes covered by the period of the lease. At no cost to the property owner, the contractors moved any improvements from the property to sites provided by the city for that purpose. Once the grade raising was completed and the canal filled, the structures would be returned to their original locations and placed on the newly raised lots. A writer for the Galveston *Daily News* minimized the expense and inconvenience. "[A]ll the property owner has to do is loan the city the use of his lot and permit the city to move his house to another lot while the grade raising project is under way and replace the house on the original property after the grade of same has been raised." The author went on to assure homeowners not in the path of the canal that the costs of raising their houses would not be excessive.

[T]he cost to the individual property owner will be small. In fact, it is said the cost of this work . . . will be reduced to a minimum, and an assurance has been given that the people of Galveston shall not be made victims of any monopoly or be compelled to pay exorbitant prices for the work . . . competition will be so great . . . that the cost of moving [or raising] houses will be reduced to the lowest notch; that even the humblest commissary house owner will be able to meet the expense and thus participate in the enhanced valuation of real estate in Galveston.

Supporters assured homeowners that fierce competition among house raisers would keep prices low.

Some residents remained skeptical. "I don't think that I have to raise the house very much" wrote Victoria W. Campbell to her daughter, "as our lot is higher than the adjoining places. but [sic] nobody can tell how it will turn out." By November of 1904, Mrs. Campbell was fearful. "When the grade raising reaches us I may be obliged to have the house raised a foot or two—and that will cost lots of money." Homeowners reluctant to raise their dwellings could fill in basements or first floors. Instead of raising their house, Charles and Florence Vedder removed partitions and flooring from the basement and built an addition onto their home at 35th Street and Avenue O when the grade raising reached their neighborhood.

Those unwilling to lease property to the city for the canal right of way or contemplating a holdout for better terms received a warning from "a member of the board" through the Galveston *Daily News*. "The board has determined that no discrimination shall be practiced. The terms of the city are fair, equitable and just. . . ."

FIGURE 3.10: E. R. Cheesborough stressed that the cost of raising a house was so minimal "that even the humblest commissary house owner will be able to meet the expense." It is unclear whether this small structure is being removed from the canal right-of-way or being raised prior to the pumping of fill. Note the outhouse entrance shielded from public view. (Courtesy Galveston County Historical Museum, Galveston, Texas.)

FIGURE 3.11: House movers from around the country flocked to Galveston during the grade raising. These particular workers are in the process of raising Grace Episcopal Church prior to fill being pumped in; thousands of jackscrews were used in the process. (Courtesy Verkin Photography Company Collection, CN 08172, Center for American History, University of Texas at Austin.)

If any are holding out . . . they will be disappointed, as the board will have the city condemn the property of every obstructionist before submitting to any unreasonable demand." Replying to C. C. Pettit in Dickinson, Texas, who refused to sign a lease because of what he perceived to be a mistaken appraisal in 1893, Captain J. P. Alvey, chairman of the Grade Raising Board, reiterated the board's strategy and suggested a certain level of frustration with those unwilling to comply with the board's requests.

What took place eleven years ago . . . is history. . . . We have no control over the city government; our duty is . . . the raising of the grade. . . . We have found in a few instances some parties attempting to hold up the Board, but in each and every instance, their demands have been made [sic] with a firm refusal. We are treating each and every one alike. . . . I understand that you have been paid for your entire lot and the little piece of ground off of the corner, concerning which we have written you, is practically of no value. . . . I presume that you have about one-fortieth of a lot and that its value can not exceed $10 and if such be the case . . . I personally, would be willing to pay you the $10 and after the grade has been raised give the land back to you as a present. . . . I think that you will hardly believe it fair to hold my Board responsible for the doings of some 'hoodlum' Board of Aldermen. In some instance a person has objected to sign a lease on account of some disagreement with the Relief Committee, another case they had been sued for taxes, another case he had at one time worked for the city and lost his job. . . . I feel sure that if, for no other reason than as a personal favor to me, you will acquiesce in our request. I certainly would dislike very much for you to do otherwise. . . .

Edmund Cheesborough was responsible for the bulk of leases. Corresponding directly with property owners or working through local realtors with information supplied by the tax assessor-collector, he eventually obtained 284 leases to lots in the canal right of way. He argued convincingly for the grade raising, appealing to the property owner's patriotic duty (as "a progressive citizen") and financial interest ("worth easily double its present value") in the same breath

and always assumed agreement with his cause ("thanking you in advance"). Female property owners were subject to the same tactics, but, in at least one case, Cheesborough sent the lease in care of a male acquaintance, "a gentleman in whom we understand you have every confidence" and who had "assured the Grade Raising Board of his friendly co-operation. . . ." As fewer and fewer leases were outstanding, he nagged the realtors to complete their tasks and account for missing leases. In a letter sent February 3, 1904, Cheesborough inquired of John Adriance the status of eleven leases yet to be obtained for the canal right-of-way, "all of the above being located within your territory."

By February 1904 Cheesborough was urging representatives of Goedhart and Bates to begin moving improvements from the canal right-of-way so that residents would understand that the project was underway and would begin raising their improvements prior to filling. In other matters, permission was secured from the U. S. Engineering Department to cut the jetty at 8th Street for the canal, and the federal government passed legislation and appropriations to extend the sea wall from 39th Street "to the end of the Government reservations at Fifty-third Street."

In the report sent to Governor Lanham in June, the board summarized its activities and breathlessly detailed the flurry of getting underway. "The bulk of the houses have been moved from the canal route. . . . About 1000 feet of the canal . . . has been completed. The draw-bridge . . . is almost completed. It is expected within ten days that all preliminaries will be finished. The first hopper-dredge is expected in this City every day; the others will follow in due course. . . . The actual work of filling, will in all probability begin about the 15th day of the present month, and from that time on will be pushed with great vigor."

When the dredge *Holm* arrived June 12, 1904, Cheesborough and the island's inhabitants expected the grade raising to move into high gear. "The bridge and funnel on the dredge was first sighted by those at the bathing pavilion a little after 4 o'clock yesterday afternoon," explained the *Daily News* in great detail, "the proximity of the little mechanical giant, calculated to play such an important part in the grade raising operations, was good tidings to the citizens of Galveston." *Holm* was the smallest of the hopper dredges used in the project. At 150 feet in length, 30 feet wide and with a draft of 13 feet, she could load 580 cubic yards of dredge material in half an hour and discharge her full capacity in forty-five minutes. Containing two engines—350 and 275 horsepower—the dredge was equipped with electric lights and directed by steam-assisted steering. The other three dredges were "of unusual size and capacity and contain features of operation different from those of any dredges heretofore used in the United States." Built in Europe for conditions much like those found in Galveston, the vessels were unusual because their hoppers could be filled and discharged with a single pump. The *Galveston*, *Leviathan*, and *Texas* could carry three times the amount of the *Holm* and would undertake the bulk of the effort to move from Galveston Bay to the streets of the city the millions of yards of fill that would be required. The dredges were built in Holland and Germany because American shipyards had never constructed such craft and lacked the skills necessary to build vessels of this design. The European-built dredges were considered ocean-going, but they made such passages at some risk. All of the ship's machinery, boilers and coal bunkers had to be placed as far aft as possible because of the space required for the hoppers. Never the most graceful of vessels, the dredges attempted to cross the Atlantic with the forward hoppers tightly battened, hoping for calm weather and flat seas. One of them, the *Texas*, went down on December 24, 1904, in a twelve-day gale off the Azores with the loss of fifteen men. The remaining crew and officers took to the lifeboats and after a harrowing thirteen days were rescued by the Italian brigantine, *Mercedes*, transferred to the steamer *Zeno*, and put ashore in Waterford.

Upon arrival in Galveston, the *Holm* began work on the grade raising canal that was essential to the plan for distributing the fill carried by the dredges. The canal was "100 feet wide on the bottom, with side slopes varying between 2 to 1 and 4 to 1, and has an average depth of 20 ft of water, with a maximum width of 200 ft at the waterline. . . . The canal had to be wide enough for the dredges to pass each other, and the waterway also contained two excavated basins so that the dredges could turn around and return to the bay for more fill material. The *Holm*, a hopper dredge, was remarkably unsuited to cutting the canal (its method was to suck material from the bottom, frequently causing the sides to cave in). At first Lindon Bates refused to consider hiring a cutting dredge to assist in digging the canal because he was angry at Chas. Clarke and Company, the local dredging firm, who threatened to oppose the foreign-built dredges. Only the most pointed letters from Cheesborough pushed him to relent.

The Holm is positively not suited for the task of digging the canal. . . . The pipeline used is composed of two kinds of pipe and the leaking is a sight to behold. . . . The work so far has unquestionably been very expensive and is costing your firm a great deal of money. It would have paid you, undoubtedly, thousands of dollars had you contracted with Mess. Clark & Co., or any one else to dig this canal using a dredge with a cutter. . . . The complaint is very bitter (and we are doing everything in our power to pacify the people) at the long delay. . . . We have pacified our citizenship and have controlled the newspapers, but fear we will not be able to continue a much greater time.

Bates finally hired Chas. Clarke and Company, and the grade raising moved more rapidly.

Bates's anger was not unfounded. Soon after the arrival of the *Holm*, Cheesborough wrote to Bates, "I am in receipt of private information which convinces me that Chas. Clark & Co., and the Atlantic, Gulf & Pacific Company, have both been doing everything in their power to prevail upon the U.S. Government to prevent the 'Holm' from going to work." Unwilling to appear as local obstructionists, Chas. Clarke & Co. mounted their opposition through "marine interests in the east to oppose the introduction of foreign dredge boats into America."

Understanding that this was a potential obstacle to the grade raising, Goedhart and Bates had tried to make the dredges as uncontroversial as possible. The boats had been sold to the

FIGURE 3.12: The *Holm* was the first of the dredges to arrive from Holland via New York. Here it proceeds through the grade raising canal at the eastern end of the island. (Courtesy Verkin Collection, Peabody Essex Museum, Salem, Massachusetts.)

company's American subsidiary and entered Galveston as American vessels. The basic issue involved violation of the Jones Act, a law passed to protect American shipping and shipbuilding interests that, among other things, prohibited foreign-built vessels from being engaged in coast-wise trade. The city of Galveston and the contractors argued that the activities of dredges and dredging did not constitute "coast-wise trade." National maritime interests believed otherwise, suggesting that the taking of dredge materials from Galveston Bay, the transportation of those materials into the canal, and the subsequent distribution of that material over the island was a form of coastal trade and was therefore included under the law. Legislation introduced in Congress attempted to prohibit such dredging activities by foreign-built craft. In addition, the opposition sought to have the laws applied retroactively to the Galveston dredges, an action that would have meant delays and considerable additional expense. City leaders and the contractors argued that no American dredges could do the job and that the savings resulting from using these particular vessels amounted to $1,500,000. In the Senate, the bill was referred to committee and not reported after that; in the House of Representatives, the bill was reported out of committee but with an amendment that exempted "any foreign-built dredge . . . now at work." No further action was taken on either measure.

With the shifting of the *Holm* to its more suitable filling duties and the subsequent arrival of the *Leviathan*, *Galveston*, and *Texas II* as well as the use of the smaller dredges *Triton* and *Nereus*, the grade raising proceeded more quickly. Quarter-mile sections of areas to be raised were enclosed by dikes. Within the encompassed area, all structures, sewers, pipes, trolley tracks, and gas lines were raised. Once everything was lifted precariously in the air, fill was pumped underneath until the grade level met that of the survey requirement.

During the time that fill was being pumped, residents negotiated the neighborhood by way of temporary catwalks and trestles, resulting in what the *Daily News* referred to as "A City on Stilts."

Galveston . . . claims the distinction of being the only city in the United States that can boast a system of elevated sidewalks. . . . On each side of the various streets are to be found temporary board walks, in many instances nothing more than planks, supported by uprights, the whole being attached by fences. They have not been built with any regard to conformity to straight lines, and their permanency is a mere question of a few weeks . . . they do not give assurance of safety to corpulently inclined gentlemen, and they are certainly not reassuring to the man with the downtown club habit.

A reporter attempting to reach the streetcar "found himself trapped. . . . Beyond was mud and water, and behind him a large discharge pipe was throwing out great quantities of filling . . . a resident . . . with the true Samaritan spirit, directed him to cross the street, walk back upon the elevated sidewalk, pass through a corner grocery and let himself down upon the dike, which led down an intersecting street to the Avenue L car line." Ad hoc arrangements abounded. The reporter noted one citizen whose property abutted the canal was obliged to tie the cow "to the railing of the back gallery . . . the barnyard fowls are privileged to roost upon the railing of the gallery mentioned and the dog and cat also inhabit that portion of the house. It is in many instances a case of 'keeping the pig in the parlor.'" Florence Vedder remembered a wedding under these circumstances.

The boardwalks, erected for the convenience of homeowners during the grade-raising, were already up, but the fill had not been turned in, so everyone prayed that the wedding day would pass without any complications. But Fate had decreed otherwise, and to the chagrin of family and friends, the fill began to pour through the pipes about 11 A.M. . . . Carriages which were to take the wedding party to Grace Church had to stop . . . two blocks away, and they all walked gingerly down the rickity boardwalks . . . it was all accepted in a spirit of fun.

There were also some advantages to the massive civil engineering

FIGURE 3.13: At its height, the grade raising employed six dredges. Here the *Nereus*, *Holm*, and *Triton* work along the canal. (Courtesy Verkin Collection, Peabody Essex Museum, Salem, Massachusetts.)

FIGURES 3.14, 3.15: Like some kind of sea serpent, pipes prowled the streets pumping fill under raised buildings. Leaking joints were a constant concern, neighborhood children ever vigilant observers. (Courtesy Verkin Photography Company Collection, CN 08173, Center for American History, University of Texas at Austin.)

FIGURE 3.16: "A City on Stilts." (Courtesy Verkin Photography Company Collection, CN 08161, Center for American History, University of Texas at Austin.)

FIGURE 3.17: Florence Vedder noted that many took advantage of the grade raising to bury unwanted "white elephants." The chairs in this image might be household detritus or a way to watch the progress of the dredge, *Triton*, through the canal. (Courtesy Verkin Collection, Peabody Essex Museum, Salem, Massachusetts.)

project. Vedder recalled that "All the housewives took the opportunity to have a general housecleaning . . . they watched trash, tin cans, broken and discarded objects disappear in the muddy fill and fast hardening sand. . . . everyone tossed in so called *white elephants*—things they had wanted to get rid of for years. Even the kitchen stove disappeared."

In his capacity as secretary to the grade raising board, Cheesborough handled the day-to-day inconveniences. He cajoled Bates into moving more quickly, pacified residents fearful of the expense, modified and canceled leases when the contractors changed the western canal terminus, and saw to the operation of pontoon bridges across the canal. He intervened when residents' services were not restored correctly and chided those in the canal right-of-way who expected the city to raise chicken houses, outhouses, and fences. In at least one case, he wrote to ask that the city attorney not bring suit against a struggling widow, Mrs. L. A. McCashin, for back taxes. What she had saved from her earnings as a seamstress she had used to raise her house; Cheesborough assured Judge Kleberg that "just as soon as she can save the money, she will adjust her taxes and a law suit will not help matters as she has no [way] outside her own labor to get funds."

Moving houses off of the canal route gave rise to new, temporary neighborhoods whose inhabitants were not always pleased with their new associates. In at least one case, Cheesborough had the contractors separate two families—the Lewises and the Leonards—because the Leonards, who were white, objected to living next to the Lewises, who were black. The Lewises, in turn, objected to being placed "alongside 'poor white trash.'" There were also problems with the dredges. Aside from the sinking of the *Texas*, there were periodic boiler problems, engine difficulties, and, worst of all, a collision between the *Nereus* and *Holm* in the canal that sank the *Holm.*

One of the most unfortunate aspects of the massive filling project was its potential effect on the island's vegetation. Obviously, any trees and plantings covered by feet of dredge material

would be killed, but even oaks or oleanders lovingly lifted by their owners along with buildings were endangered. Since the fill was 15 to 45 percent sand and the rest saltwater, the resulting soil composition was not suited to grow much of anything. The *Daily News* lamented the loss:

As is well known to every one who knows the arboricultural beauty of the city, there are hundreds and hundreds of the most beautiful tropical shade and ornamental trees . . . hundreds, perhaps, of stately palms and wide-branched live oaks . . . the effect of the salt upon a large percentage of the trees will prove disastrous.

Victoria Campbell wrote her daughter Alice about the problem: "Our old home never looked so sweet desirable [sic] and shady as it does this spring. The house and fence and everything is on stilts which of course is disfiguring, but the palms the elms and Oleanders are simply beautiful it is distressing to know that after the filling is put in the trees will all die and the place will look as desolate as the desert of Arizona." Many letters of inquiry were sent to leading botanists and landscape architects throughout the country. A reply received from George E. Kessler, chief landscape architect for the Louisiana Purchase Exposition at St. Louis, recommended that the trees and shrubs to be saved be moved only once, lifted immediately prior to fill being pumped in, and replaced upon completion. He specified the kinds of wagons and tools to use and sent photographs illustrating the process. Some residents built protective wooden walls around their trees and raised them using topsoil or dirt from other parts of the island, the mainland, or even overseas. "All up and down Broadway chaos reigns," wrote Victoria Campbell, "people are digging dirt from esplanades and street to fill their yards rather than have the sand. . . ." Dr. Randall, a neighbor of the Campbells, "has raised about eight feet and is filling his yard himself with South American soil mostly it comes to Galveston as ballast. . . ." Even the city tried to mitigate the damage. Where street surface soil was "of a loamy substance or well compacted earth," it was to be scraped off and deposited at intersections to be put back over the newly graded thoroughfares. Most of the live oaks, oleanders, and tropical vegetation on the east end of the island today date to replacement efforts after the storm and grade raising.

The Women's Health Protective Association (WHPA) took the revegetation of the island as one of its missions during this time. The need for replanting the island in the course of the grade raising coincided with national campaigns for city beautification, and the women found sources of support among national "City Beautiful" organizations. The WHPA quickly began the process of finding replacements for trees and shrubs lost during the filling of the island. They consulted agricultural experts, obtained cuttings and seedlings, and convinced the railroads to carry thousands of palm trees without charge from California and Florida. Beginning with parks and boulevards most heavily utilized by residents and visitors to Galveston, the WHPA worked its way throughout the raised area and encouraged other groups and organizations to take responsibility for the replanting of their buildings and grounds. The WHPA operated a nursery and gave away or sold at cost seeds, rose bushes, oleander cuttings, and other plants to property owners wanting to restore their home gardens. Contests were held, and prizes awarded to acknowledge residents' efforts to beautify recently raised structures and lots. For several years, starting in 1906, annual horse shows funded WHPA civic improvement programs, and the event quickly became a focal point of the social season on the island. When the shows ceased in 1910—largely due to the advent of the automobile and an absence of horses to show—organizers could claim great success from their efforts.

In all, 2,156 structures of various kinds were raised during the course of the filling. The most spectacular of these was St. Patrick's Catholic Church, one of the largest churches in the city at that time. Located at 34th Street and Avenue K, it measured 53 feet by 140 feet and was estimated to weigh approximately 3,000 tons, its tower alone accounting for 1,400 tons. The church was lifted from its foundation by excavation underneath and placed in a cradle of heavy timbers and iron girders. Seven hundred jackscrews were then distributed under the cradle, and the structure was very slowly and carefully raised five feet. "Owing to the nature of the construction of this building," wrote the *Daily News*, "fears were entertained as to the feasibility of raising it. It is virtually a big brick shell with the exception of the solidly constructed tower." The paper went on to observe, "No accidents occurred during the operation and services have never been discontinued while the raising was in progress. On St. Patrick's Day, March 17, a record-breaking congregation attended the services while the church was elevated high in the air." Ursuline Convent, another monumental religious structure, was deemed too large to raise, so the first floor was filled instead.

Work continued, slowly and steadily, for years. By September 26, 1906, the halfway mark had been reached, but in February of 1907, the contractors requested and received a three-year extension on the time for completion. In 1910 North American Dredging Company took over the contract and pumped sand from Offat's Bayou to finish the work. Goedhart and Bates claimed to have lost four hundred thousand dollars on the project, but they received the praises of a grateful city. When the work was over in 1911, five hundred blocks had been filled with 16.3 million cubic yards of sand. Other parts of the island have been filled as development has moved west, but nothing has been done of the magnitude of this initial effort. In January 1904 E. R. Cheesborough contacted W. H. Plummer in Millbridge, Maine, to secure a lease for the canal right-of-way. "The Grade Raising Board," he wrote, "is doing everything that mortal men can do to succeed in their stupendous undertaking, and we believe that success is assured."

Constructing the sea wall and raising the city's grade—projects that were inextricably interrelated—brought with them a host of environmental ramifications. Raising the grade was pointless without building a wall to protect the newly high ground from washing away into the Gulf. And the wall was essential to block potentially

FIGURE 3.18: The WHPA worked diligently to replace the tropical foliage lost to the storm and grade raising. Through annual horse shows, the women's organization raised funds to revegetate the island. (Courtesy Rosenberg Library, Galveston, Texas.)

FIGURE 3.19: The largest structure raised—St. Patrick's Catholic Church— is located at 35th Street and Broadway. (Courtesy Verkin Photography Company Collection, CN 08154, Center for American History, University of Texas at Austin.)

FIGURE 3.20: The Letitia Rosenberg Women's Home was another major public structure raised during this time. Note the removal of stairs at the front and the ramping to afford access. No doubt John Egert viewed the event as an excellent opportunity to advertise his expertise as a house "mover and raiser." (Courtesy Verkin Collection, Peabody Essex Museum, Salem, Massachusetts.)

FIGURE 3.21: As surreal as boats among buildings and a concrete barricade replacing the natural division of sand and water, constructing the sea wall and completing the grade raising had environmental ramifications only guessed at in the early twentieth century. While both civil engineering feats have protected the city's structures, surrounding beaches and wetlands have paid the price. (Courtesy Verkin Collection, Peabody Essex Museum, Salem, Massachusetts.)

destructive wave damage from future storms. As noted, however, the wall was quickly undermined due to the extensive erosion of the Gulf-side beaches. Rock groins, added years after the fact, do help accrue and retain sand in front of the wall, but city leaders are faced with the prospect of eternal vigilance—and expense—if they want to keep beaches for tourists and protection for residents. In addition, the effects of Galveston's various jetties, groins, and sea wall extend to beaches both east and west, where ongoing erosion processes threaten later twentieth-century development. Galveston learned early on what the rest of coastal America is only now comprehending: barrier islands, while magical spaces, are not necessarily appropriate for significant human habitation.

Even as Galveston struggled throughout that first, agonizing year of recovery, city leaders took a long, hard look at the island's future and made decisions that they believed were essential for its survival. A dramatic change in government assured investors and calmed critics of earlier administrations, and the sea wall and grade raising guaranteed protection from future hurricanes. Its political and physical infrastructure restored, Galveston's male leadership concentrated on creating the best possible business climate. But the restoration process created more than just fertile ground for economic growth. Galveston's path through the next decade was unquestionably shaped by the city's experience of disaster and recovery.

CHAPTER FOUR

"To attain that superior success"
Recovery and Growth

Galveston City is several acres of people, mainly optimists safe-guarding a community of interests, endowed with grit, persistency, an abiding faith in their ultimate destiny and a notion that theirs is the best place on earth.

WILLIAM PHARES CHOCHRAN

MOST GALVESTONIANS basked in the notion that commission government was not only innovative but also successful. Five hundred small- to medium-sized cities—mostly in the Midwest—seized the idea and changed their own municipal government structures. If imitation is the highest form of flattery, then Deep Water Committee members, white businessmen, and members of the Women's Health Protective Association should have been blushing with pride. National magazines touted the new form of government; would-be city reformers came to Galveston to see how it worked and to take home suggestions; curious muckrakers continued to keep an eye on commissioners' honesty, integrity, and industry. Only a minority knew what most Americans wanted to ignore—that commission government was something short of democratic with its at-large elections that eliminated opportunity for black officeholders.

Still, the efficiency of the five commissioners brought paeans of praise from city boosters. By 1908 Commissioner Isaac H. Kempner had achieved new credit worthiness in city financing. He saved the city from bankruptcy, retired the floating debt, and made sure that grade raising bonds—by then close to $2 million—were paid on schedule. The city had had no credit rating in 1900; it now stood at A1. All this occurred with the sea wall and grade raising programs under way. Good credit and progress on the grade raising sent the city into a modernizing frenzy. Officials spent $158,000 in four years (1904–1908) on paving forty-nine city blocks with vitrified bricks, and boosters bragged that before commission government

FIGURE 4.1: Panorama of Galveston in 1910 after the grade raising. In the distance are the ship channel and the wharves. The domed structure on the left is Ball High School facing Avenue G. The church to the right is Trinity Episcopal Church on 22nd Street. In the park stands a monument, probably a drinking fountain donated to the city by Henry Rosenberg in 1893. The double steeples in the center are the spires of St. Mary's Cathedral on 21st Street. To the right is 20th Street intersecting Avenue F (Winnie) in the foreground. (Courtesy Rosenberg Library, Galveston, Texas.)

there had been but eight blocks of brick pavement in the entire city. To add to the improved appearance, in the same four years the city spent nearly one hundred thousand dollars surfacing with crushed rock and mud shell forty or more street blocks mainly in the residential sections. Finally, following the advice of sanitary expert Dr. George A. Soper, commissioners spent more than eighty-five thousand dollars on new storm drains (badly needed since the grade raising made the old drains inaccessible), raised water mains, improved the water pumping plant at Alta Loma on the mainland, and repaired public property and buildings. As historian Harold M. Hyman discovered, creative financing, including an out-of-court settlement with the Galveston Wharf Company for more than sixty-two thousand dollars,

won Galveston . . . a rebuilt and enlarged urban infrastructure[,] . . . new schools, water and sewer systems, a repaired city hall and other municipal buildings, resurfaced streets for the business district and several residential sections (including for the first time some predominantly black neighborhoods), modernized police and firefighting equipment, . . . and the growing commerce brought in on the Intracoastal Canal.

The year 1912 proved to be a record-breaking one for Galveston. Department of Commerce and Labor reports announced that Galveston had once again become the second port of the United States, meaning that the value of its exports and imports exceeded that of New Orleans, Philadelphia, San Francisco, and Boston, and that it was bested only by New York City. City directory editors gloated unabashedly as they communicated the news to avid readers: "The business of the city transacted through her banks, business houses and over her wharves has been, during the past year, the greatest in her history. . . . The year 1912 was a record-breaker in every respect. . . ." In fact, Galveston was the leading cotton port of the world—at 4,267,577 bales it shipped three times more cotton than any other port that year. The city's total import and export figures were valued at nearly $292 million—$286 million in exports, mainly cotton, cottonseed oil and meal, meat-packing products, and lumber; and $6 million in imports, an increase of $2 million for imports in one year. To say that the city exported more than it imported was a huge understatement and presented problems of disproportion. But by 1914, imports had increased to nearly $9 million due in part to President Woodrow Wilson and the Underwood Tariff, which reduced federal tariffs on selected products. That year Galveston, in an odd reversal, received three thousand head of cattle from Mexico and 1.5 million bushels of corn from Argentina. Bananas, coffee, tea, jute, sugar, liquors, and toys from around the world managed to land at Galveston's docks. Passenger liners headed to Europe filled with traveling southwesterners who would arrive in Liverpool in just two weeks time.

The reason exports and imports were so high went back to that awful night in September 1900 when the wharves lay in splinters and vessels were found toppled and trapped miles to the north. Since that time the wharves, with an initial investment of five hundred thousand dollars from the Galveston Wharf Company, had been reconstructed with berthing space for over one hundred ships; the rebuilt piers covered five miles of water frontage and were worth $15 million. Southern Pacific Railroad, whose wharves had been the most heavily damaged, rebuilt and added a one-million-bushel grain elevator and tracks that brought cars directly shipside. With sixty acres of warehouse space, expanded silos, and improved grain elevators, Galveston boasted one of the most modern port facilities in the nation. This attracted producers in the Midwest, whose expanded population, increased production of cattle and grains, and carefully orchestrated links to Galveston—the principal deep water port for Texas and states to the north—brought increased shipping traffic.

The hurricane of 1900 put the city back on the federal agenda as a site for jetty and harbor improvements, as a base for military defense, and for an immigration station. Thanks to the supporters of deep water and their success in acquiring federal funding, the channel to the bay was deepened to thirty-two feet clearance. Consequently, huge naval battleships plied routinely into Galveston

FIGURE 4.2: City streets paved with vitrified bricks, sidewalks, and prosperous looking store fronts all testified to the partial economic recovery of Galveston after the storm and the grade raising. In this 1913 street scene, commerce appears healthy. (Courtesy Rosenberg Library, Galveston, Texas.)

FIGURE 4.3: The Galveston wharves in 1912 included berthing space for over one hundred ships, five miles of water frontage worth $15 million, sixty acres of warehouse space, expanded silos, and improved grain elevators, making Galveston the leading cotton port in the world and the second leading trade port in the nation. This photograph published in 1915 shows the harbor looking west from Pier 19. (Courtesy Rosenberg Library, Galveston, Texas.)

harbor, staying a week to ten days. No doubt the impending completion of the Panama Canal would give Galveston an edge as an embarkation point for naval vessels as well as for midwestern goods bound for the West Coast. To this end, Deep Water Committee members lobbied federal regulatory commissioners for reduced freight rates from cities in the Midwest to Houston and Galveston. Then, anticipating trade—bananas, coffee, and tourism—through the canal and with all parts of Latin America, investors pushed for shipping lines such as the Lykes Steamship Company to establish headquarters in Galveston. Stormy relations with Mexico (the U.S. would be warring with its neighbor in 1916) promoted Galveston as the nearest port for military mobilization. Fort Crockett at the western end of the city was part of this fortification. Congress appropriated four hundred thousand dollars to rebuild Fort Crockett, a two-company coast artillery post at the western end of the island. In addition it sent a brigade of four thousand to staff the artillery companies and to provide provisional regiments of infantrymen. The thirty-building fort was useful both as a base for conducting drills and maneuvers and as a possible deterrent to violations of the neutrality laws on the Mexican border.

A $125,000 immigration station on Pelican Island, in the midst of Galveston harbor, served as a conduit for mostly European arrivals to the United States. The Galveston Movement, under the sponsorship of the Jewish Immigrants' Information Bureau—promoted by Jacob Schiff in New York and aided by Galveston's Rabbi Henry Cohen—brought some ten thousand immigrants through Galveston and then by train to points in the Midwest. The plan envisioned routing Jews away from congested eastern cities and into the heartland of the United States. Although few arrivals stayed in Galveston, the immigration traffic prompted new employment and services such as water, electricity, and telephone lines to a little used part of the city. Unfortunately, short-sighted citizens objected to Galveston becoming a "dumping place" for immigrants, and these hardworking newcomers—who would have increased the city's population, spent money on goods and services, and created a wider tax base—went elsewhere. Next to the immigration station the

FIGURE 4.4: The causeway, built in 1912, spanned the two-mile stretch of Galveston Bay from the mainland to Galveston Island. Built on concrete pilings, its 154-foot-wide bridge allowed space for two railroads, an electric Houston-to-Galveston interurban train, and auto traffic. (Courtesy Rosenberg Library, Galveston, Texas.)

FIGURE 4.5: An engineering marvel for its time, the rolling lift bridge at the center of the causeway raised upward one hundred feet to allow for the passage of boats across Galveston Bay. (Courtesy Rosenberg Library, Galveston, Texas.)

federal government built a thirty-thousand-dollar life-saving station and across the bay a federal quarantine station, adding dollars to the local economy.

The third great engineering project of the post-storm era, after the sea wall and the grade raising, was construction in 1912 of a 10,642-foot multilane, multipurpose causeway, consisting of roadway, arch bridge, and lift bridge, which spanned the two-mile stretch of bay from the mainland to Galveston Island. Built on concrete pilings driven ten to sixteen feet below the bottom of the bay, it boasted a 154-foot-wide roadbed for two railroads, an electric interurban train, and early automobiles—including Model A Fords, Chevrolets, and Packards—that could speed across the bay. A rolling lift bridge raised skyward to give a clear waterway of one hundred feet for ships.

Galveston had been connected to the mainland by a number of bridges since 1860. Railroad bridges were added in 1877 and 1896, but the 1900 storm destroyed every island link with the mainland. The 1912 project, which cost nearly $1.5 million, was financed by Galveston County, the railroads, and the interurban. The Galveston-Houston Electric Railway, the interurban, shuttled passengers between the cities in approximately one hour and twenty minutes and cost $1.25 one way, $2.00 round trip. Nothing could have been better for Galveston's burgeoning tourist industry or for the export of cotton and other materials. And the county helped by adding five hundred thousand dollars worth of good roads on the mainland so that tourists, truck farmers, and tradesmen could reach the causeway and the island.

Just about the time the causeway was nearing completion, a handful of Galveston businessmen—Commissioner Isaac Kempner, Bertrand Adoue, John Sealy, and H. S. Cooper—financed the construction of the city's second major hotel—the Hotel Galvez. The city needed more lodgings for tourists, and the $1.5 million, six-story, 250-room resort structure located on newly finished Sea Wall Boulevard now rivaled the venerable Tremont, which, not to be outdone, decided to spend one hundred thousand dollars on renovations.

Galveston's beaches, now visible from atop the seventeen-foot-high sea wall, had long been a sandy playground for the state's vacationers. Cool breezes, an azure blue gulf, normally small swells, and 80-degree water invited thousands of tourists each year, giving Galveston another source of income beyond shipping.

The city needed to begin looking elsewhere for income. Despite all efforts, new businesses were shy about locating in such a precarious position, and the world was well aware of Galveston's devastation after the hurricane. Laborers could not be enticed to the island at first because they feared the city's vulnerability; it was this fear that shut down the cotton bagging and rope mills, Isaac Kempner reasoned. What Kempner had forgotten was that laborers had begun leaving Galveston in 1895 during the depression, when mill exploitation of labor reached its nadir with thirteen-hour days at low pay. Mill workers begged the church ladies' aid societies to give them the money to leave town. Yet, the closing of the mills did present problems for Galveston by reducing its economic diversification. The hurricane had changed industrial investors' and laborers' perceptions of the city's future.

By 1908, however, with the security of a sea wall and the possibility of work continuing after the grade raising, Galveston's working-class men and women found a hearty welcome. By 1910, workers had organized thirty-two unions, nine of which were established after the storm. A sizable leap in union activity came between 1910 and 1914, when the city directory listed fifty-one unions. Among the newcomers were two unions that reflected the turn in Galveston's labor needs since the dredging of the bay and the construction of the causeway—the International Association of Bridge and Structural Iron Workers, and the Dredgeboat Men, Tugboat Men, Bargemen, Fishermen, Oystermen, Piledriver Men, and Scowmen's Union. The screwmen, who had skillfully squeezed 15 percent more cotton into the holds of ships, found themselves gradually displaced by the invention and perfection of the cotton compress. As early as 1900, high-density compressing machines could inexpensively squeeze a bale to the weight of thirty-two pounds per cubic foot, eliminating the need for manual compacting in the holds of ships. Membership in the Screwmen's Benevolent Association (SBA) declined from a high of 588 in 1904 to a low of 350 by 1920. Many screwmen were reduced to loading cotton, but even those jobs decreased as mechanized stowing tools replaced workers. The screwmen survived as a longshoreman's union, loading and unloading cargo, but their once vaunted power on the docks disappeared. Black and white screwmen vied for the work, and in 1913, when jobs were declining, the two racially separated unions attempted amalgamation in order to have better bargaining power with shipping companies. But this failed when several shipping companies offered exclusive contracts to the white union, leaving black screwmen and longshoremen to work as they had before on separate docks and with separate companies. To complicate

matters, the shipping industry, from which Galveston's wealth had derived, would slowly decline along with the need for large numbers of longshoremen and stevedores.

The dredging of deep water channels was no longer limited to cities like Galveston. An increase in federal support for such capital investment and improved technology made deep water harbors an attainable goal for most coastal cities, and the Galveston Wharf Company had few friends among shipping interests along the coast. The halcyon days of the Galveston Wharf Company would gradually fade before the city's premier rival, Houston, which dredged and widened Buffalo Bayou and created its own deep water ship channel in 1914. Oil and petroleum processing, which had been a boon for towns like Beaumont and Houston, bypassed

FIGURE 4.6: The Hotel Galvez, shown here at its opening in 1911, boasted six stories, 250 rooms, and an unparalleled view of the Gulf. It cost $1.5 million and pushed its rival, the Tremont Hotel, to spend $100,000 remodeling. (Courtesy Prints and Photographs Division, Library of Congress, Washington, D.C.)

Galveston, which at the time of the Spindletop gusher in 1901 was struggling with its recovery. Population statistics showed a slow growth pattern, and indeed, Galveston never did catch up to the three larger cities in Texas (Dallas, Houston, and San Antonio) after the hurricane.

Still, Galveston had charm that was enhanced by its good weather, sandy beaches, and historical appeal. The Cotton Carnival and Exposition, first organized in 1908 by the Galveston Business League, became *the* summer event on the island. Its initial purpose was to attract cotton agents to Galveston so they could see for themselves the port and the city's advantages. Extending from eleven to eighteen days, the carnival provided "recreation, entertainment, and instruction of which many[,] many thousands of people throughout the interior have availed themselves." The carnival was also useful for promoting the "clean, healthful recreative properties of the Treasure Island" to beach lovers and sojourners. And in the spirit of the Progressive Era, citizens hoped that by attracting tourist dollars, the city would continue to clean up its debris-ridden alleys, replant the island, and safeguard the beaches—goals that women civic activists shared as well. When the Galveston Business League, the Chamber of Commerce, and the Greater Galveston Publicity Committee merged to form the Galveston Commercial Association in 1911, boosterism reached a new high. From the proceeds of the Commercial Association's fund drives, which annually brought in fifty thousand dollars, members promoted commerce and recreation—shipping, wholesale and

FIGURE 4.7: Dressed in their finery, visiting strollers enjoy the beach at low tide in 1913. The sea wall towers above them. (Courtesy Rosenberg Library, Galveston, Texas.)

FIGURE 4.8: Galveston's beaches had long been a sandy playground for the state's vacationers. Cool breezes, an azure blue gulf, normally small swells, and 80-degree water invited thousands of tourists each year. Here bathers enjoy the Gulf on a warm day in June 1914. (Courtesy Prints and Photographs Division, Library of Congress, Washington, D.C.)

retail merchandising, insurance, labor, real estate, and agricultural development on the mainland as well as conventions, carnivals, beachfront development, and band concerts on the beach. Unadvertised, but well known to anyone familiar with Galveston, was the thriving red light district located on Postoffice Street on the west side of Rosenberg Avenue. For years college students made Galveston the site of their spring breaks largely because of the beach and "the district." Indeed, tourists jokingly pointed to the Texas Heroes Monument in the middle of Broadway and Rosenberg as indicating the way not to the San Jacinto battlefield but to the bordellos on the north side of town.

As an outgrowth of the Cotton Carnival's success with its summertime parades, boosters calling themselves the Kotton Karnival Kids (K.K.K.) found another way to exploit the usually balmy early spring weather and bring tourists to the island. Capitalizing on the city's large Catholic population, which reached fifteen thousand in 1906, organizers reintroduced Mardi Gras festivities in 1910. The city's first Mardi Gras celebration dated back to 1867, but events were discontinued due to expense in the 1880s. The first really memorable renewed Mardi Gras came in 1914, when the K.K.K. (in 1920 they changed the initials to M.M.M.—Mystic Merry Makers) held a dance and costume contest at the old beach auditorium at 27th and Avenue Q. Unseasonable snow that year prevented the parade, but in 1915, 1,200 people attended the dance held at the Grand Opera House. Mardi Gras may have enticed few tourists to the city, but it was a spectacle that residents long remembered. Margaret Sealy Burton, who grew up in "Open Gates," one of Galveston's finest mansions, recalled that "the invitations were sent out in grand splendor" with

the blast of the long coach horn, from the trumpeter that stood at the back of the golden coach drawn by six snow white horses, as it dashed up to each favored door. The herald, who delivered the golden card . . . was dressed in red velvet; the postillions were in silver cloth[,] and the King, as he sat inside, was [a] triumph in Turquoise satin, embroidered in heavily precious jewels. In one gloved hand he held a scepter, and

upon his reddish curls rested a diamond crown. It was a regular Cinderella coach, and lucky was the maiden to be home, as the coach stopped at the door. . . .

This attempt to bring tourist dollars to Galveston grew out of the city's need to diversify its economy, and ultimately it became far more successful than the No-Tsu-Oh! (Houston spelled backwards) festivals that Galveston's chief rival put on to attract business. Mardi Gras has been reinstated and continues in even more expansive and elaborate form today.

Efforts to enhance the commercial life of the city were complemented by the planting and beautification program of the Women's Health Protective Association (WHPA), mentioned earlier. The WHPA, in turn, inspired other Progressive Era organizations—the Galveston Business League, the Galveston Commercial Association, the Young Men's Business Association, the Child Conservation League, the Juvenile Protective Association, the Playground Association, the Young Women's Health Protective Association, the Jewish Council of Women, a reorganized Woman's Christian Temperance Union (WCTU), the Young Women's Christian Association (YWCA), and Mothers' Clubs (eventually the PTA)—which looked for ways to improve the schools through such amenities as playgrounds and parks, hot lunches, school nurses, and artwork on schoolroom walls. The Business League, among its many projects, promoted better lighting for the city, and, when it merged as part of the Commercial Association, the new group took out associate membership in the WHPA and cooperated in civic projects. The Jewish Council of Women, founded in 1910 to help recent Jewish arrivals from Europe, sponsored a free kindergarten for Jewish immigrant children in 1913. Elizabeth Kempner bought and donated most of the playground and indoor equipment for the school on the grounds of Temple B'nai Israel. The Child Conservation League, guided by physician Ethel Lyon Heard, conducted Better Baby Conferences to help reduce infant mortality. The WCTU—both black and white unions—made sure that students and soldiers at Fort Crockett knew about the evils of alcohol. But it was a hard sell because Galveston was a city full of European immigrants from Germany, Ireland, England, Italy, and France, who appreciated the fact that Galveston had its own brewery and beer gardens. The Galveston YWCA, founded in 1914, promoted the protection and welfare of young working girls coming to the city. Its members provided a cafeteria, a dormitory for lodging, a gymnasium with athletic classes, and an employment bureau. The well-established Young Men's Christian Association (YMCA) and various other organizations also set their sights on reaching citizens. Thus a Progressive Era clubbiness developed that fostered cooperation and shared goals for community improvement. The sea wall, the grade raising, and the causeway allowed Galvestonians to believe that technological changes meant progress for the city. Progressive reformers, on the other hand, counterbalanced technology with innovative community programs that went beyond planting trees and selling rose bushes.

In the years between 1912 and 1915 the WHPA became something of a gadfly organization to city hall and to city entrepreneurs. In its efforts to promote civic improvements, it devised multiple departments devoted to all areas of public health and child welfare. Sanitation remained a basic concern: citizens were warned about the dangers of germs spread through public spitting (it was against the law) and carried by flies. With horse and cattle manure as well as compost heaps and garbage still very much an urban problem, flies were a constant headache and screens on windows were a rarity. WHPA members conducted a "Swat the Fly" campaign and placed trash cans in convenient locations. They promoted private incinerators for the burning of trash and sought clean streets and alleys. They objected to billboards, smoke from the electric powerhouse, cattle and horses let out to graze on recently planted yards, and a lack of building codes for newly built housing. Social concerns cropped up as well; WHPA members wanted a woman elected to the schoolboard (they were successful in 1917), public women's restrooms downtown and on the beaches, and silent zones surrounding hospitals. They improved conditions for children by establishing a visiting nurse association, well-baby clinics, hot lunches in the schools, regular medical examination of schoolchildren, better parks and playgrounds, and a neighborhood (settlement) house in the West End where they maintained programs and kept statistics on children's welfare. Under the leadership of their president, Jean Scrimgeour Morgan, the WHPA began the sale of Christmas seals for the prevention and cure of tuberculosis. By 1913 Galveston had its own center—the Walter Colquitt Memorial Children's Hospital for Bone and Glandular Tuberculosis. WHPA members continued their work of city planting, making Galveston a beautiful city once again; and to raise money for all their projects, they held bake contests, band concerts, and "Seed Days."

Of all the programs, projects, and activities of the WHPA, the one that had the most profound impact was their campaign for pure food and milk. It was also the toughest to launch and brought the WHPA into direct conflict with city commission government—after ten years of cooperation. The struggle lasted over five years and prompted lawsuits, inspection committees, and state intervention. It pushed these white middle-class women into politics as nothing else had before, and in their anger and frustration over an intransigent city commission, they saw clearly their own impotence and the value of the vote. This battle made suffragists out of most of them.

It all started with the completion of the grade raising. Once the sand, water, and mess began to vanish, and WHPA plantings returned dignity and beauty to the city, women forged ahead with an agenda that included issues of cleanliness in markets, restaurants, bakeries, and dairies. They entered this new phase in 1912 by seeking enforcement of existing city and state laws and enactment of new ordinances in places where food was prepared for public consumption. In the days before routine health department inspections and posted grades, there were few safeguards on the quality of food. The rule was caveat emptor—let the buyer beware. But the women reformers took the threat to the health and safety of the populace—not to mention their own families—very seriously. Surely, the city health department could do better than it had done.

This determination to end the purveyance of bad food in dirty

FIGURE 4.9: A shady sidewalk looking east on Broadway Boulevard. The Women's Health Protective Association planted trees, shrubs, and flowering bushes, mainly oleanders, along public streets. The revegetation of the is- land and the WHPA campaign for improved sidewalks and clean streets and alleys made Galveston a more attractive city after the grade raising. (Courtesy Rosenberg Library, Galveston, Texas.)

establishments brought WHPA members in direct conflict with city commissioners; the campaign became heated and confrontational primarily because the WHPA held a different philosophy toward governance. As with many progressives, they believed that government should protect consumers from unhealthy or unclean products through regulation. Commissioners, on the other hand, were more interested in protecting free enterprise with as few regulations and as little interference as possible. While the commission form of government may have been innovative and its members dutiful and diligent in helping to revive the city's credit rating and economic future, its officials were dismally behind the times with regard to enforcement of pure food and milk laws. WHPA members meant to bring them into the twentieth century on that issue, and the new form of municipal government helped the women in their task. Commissioners were far more accessible to elite and middle-class white women than aldermen had been in the days before municipal reform. For the previous ten years, WHPA members had worked with the commissioners to recover from the hurricane and to beautify the city. They knew their way around city hall, and they knew how to put pressure on its inhabitants—some WHPA members were married to commissioners, others were family members. Consanguinity proved useful in the fight for pure food and milk.

Monthly WHPA meetings bristled with member reports and citizen complaints about the status of the city's sanitation: ptomaine poisonings, trash in streets and alleys, and poor garbage collection, which prompted one critic to ask the WHPA "to stir up the health department in that direction." Citizens saw little use in going directly to city authorities; the WHPA was a much better clearinghouse for those kinds of complaints. These requests empowered the women of the WHPA to do battle for the good of the community.

Thus, in 1913, the WHPA, in concert with the Galveston Commercial Association, asked Dr. J. P. Simonds, head of preventive medicine at the Medical Department of the University of Texas in Galveston, to conduct a sanitation survey for the city. Many cities in the Northeast and Midwest used sanitation surveys to identify and correct their major health problems. The result of Galveston's survey was a thirty-page report, the first of its kind in Texas. It showed that the city's water purity was good, but it listed problems in housing (deemed "deplorable" because of no building codes); garbage collection (labeled "astounding" in the infrequency of collection); and the sewer system ("not up to the best standard of efficiency"). Public schools needed to abolish the public drinking cup and begin regular medical examinations and vaccinations of students; playgrounds were inadequate; and stagnant pools of water provided a breeding ground for mosquitoes, while alleys and streets needed better cleaning (despite the fact that there was a commissioner whose sole responsibility was streets and alleys). Markets, bakeries, and groceries were "in serious need of improvement."

Dr. Simonds and his team of medical students saved their most scathing remarks for the quality of the city's milk supply and its dairymen, who were among the worst offenders. Milk, the report stated, was "an essential article of food; one that is probably accountable for more sickness and more deaths than all other foods put together." Galveston's milk had so much dirt in it that you could often see it at the bottom of the bottles. The survey reported flies in the bottling room, manure from the sides of the cow in the milk, and unsanitary bottling methods. In one case a boy held milk bottles under a flowing spout; the overflow went into a bucket. "When this bucket became full, this milk in which the boy had practically washed his hands was poured back into the large can, bottled and sold." These practices resulted in enormous bacteria levels in the milk that children consumed and led to high rates of infant mortality. Tuberculosis, typhoid fever, infant cholera, dehydration caused by diarrhea, and death were the outcome of bad milk, and Galveston's children were the victims. The sanitation survey became the most important tool the WHPA could have fashioned; they used it like a crowbar to open the door to better regulation of milk and food.

The technology for assuring good milk—pasteurizing and checking for skimming or added water—was already well known by 1913. Moreover, Texas had passed the Pure Food and Drug Act in 1907, which was complemented by city ordinances passed in 1906 and 1907. Twenty-seven cities had created milk commissions to regulate local dairies, and by 1910 the American Public Health Association had published standard methods for the bacterial testing of milk. This brought into being the National Commission of Milk Standards, which set testing procedures for city health departments. None of these standards were in evidence in Galveston—no pasteurized or graded milk and no hope of getting these safeguards unless citizens bombarded city officials. The city health department lacked sufficient inspectors, and WHPA members threatened to take on the task of inspection themselves.

Dr. Walter Kleberg, head of the city health department, was by then under public scrutiny, and he soon began investigating bakeries and dairies for himself. He took with him the city food inspector, several officers from the WHPA, and reporters. They visited fourteen bakeries and discovered that they ranged from

the carelessly insanitary to the unspeakably filthy. . . . Pans into which dozens of eggs had been broken, small wooden tubs containing jam and the "filler" for pies, brushes, used for glazing with eggs and sugar . . . greasy rags . . . and cake tins were found in various establishments, and in some instances were black with flies.

The inspectors photographed it all—bread, toilets, stables, flies—and gave the bakers a crash course in hygiene, but not one baker lost a license. The dairies were next; city officials, again accompanied by the WHPA milk committee, discovered that conditions had not improved since the survey went out. No citations were issued, even though forty-two of forty-seven dairies bottled milk with dirt and sand in it. Half of the milk inspected exceeded the bacteria count of one hundred thousand bacteria per cubic centimeter. City commissioners, when told this, said they preferred to educate rather than penalize the dairymen.

A bright spot in the battle for pure milk came when the health department hired Dr. Ethel Lyon Heard (who became president of

FIGURE 4.10. Jean Scrimgeour Morgan was president of the Women's Health Protective Association (WHPA) from 1908 to 1912 and 1914 to 1915. She favored health inspection of all establishments where food was prepared, regardless of the social class of the owners. WHPA members called for measures that protected public health over commercialism or class solidarity. (Courtesy Rosenberg Library, Galveston, Texas.)

the WHPA in 1916) as pathologist for testing milk samples. A physician and a club woman, she was able to bridge the concerns of the medical community with those of the WHPA, help the WHPA publicize the results of her samplings, and take a solid case for reform to the city commissioners. Meanwhile, WHPA members printed the statistics compiled by Dr. Heard and made sure that every consumer received a copy in hopes that bad publicity would bring change. But conditions worsened. In 1914, Dr. W. S. Carter, dean of the State Medical College, researched Galveston's milk and found that one quarter of the samplings had bacteria levels of over one million per cubic centimeter, while half had visible dirt. "We are exactly where we were six years ago when the city adopted its milk ordinance. . . . I don't know of a single case of revoking a milk license in the six years since we have had our milk ordinance."

No action on the part of the city led to more investigations by WHPA members of dairies, meat markets, bakeries, and even restaurants. The WHPA tried to be even-handed in its inspections, seeking to grade all food establishments according to their level of hygiene, regardless of the class, race, or ethnicity of the owners. Initially, however, there was debate in the WHPA about the issue of inspecting hotel kitchens controlled by elite whites. The newly built Hotel Galvez, with its elegant restaurant, was owned by members of the Deep Water Committee and Commissioner Isaac Kempner, for example. Did the "ladies" have the right to inspect hotel kitchens in upper-crust establishments? One reformer argued, "The association must stand for protection against all bad food, and must not discriminate in favor of hotels and restaurants when the inspection of groceries, bakeries and other establishments is going on." Otherwise, she continued, "the whole work of the association would be useless. . . ." Some in the organization objected to WHPA members marching into a kitchen owned by Galveston's elites, although they had no hesitation in doing the same to small grocerymen, bakers, and dairymen. The obvious class bias that attended the discussion angered the majority of WHPA members, who in February 1914 elected Jean Scrimgeour Morgan as their president. Morgan, who had been president from 1908 to 1912, favored inspec-

tion of all establishments where food was prepared. At this point it became clear that health and protection were far more important to these middle- and upper-class women than allegiance to class status or to city authorities. For them social welfare superseded profits. WHPA members broke ranks with the male members of their class and called for measures that protected life—issues that were most important to these women.

Thus restaurant and hotel kitchens joined the list of establishments inspected by the WHPA. Committee visits led to reports: they published lists in the newspaper, exposing the good and the bad; they led boycotts against dirty food stores, bakeries, and dairies; they printed and posted their own standards for food vendors; they enlisted the support of men's organizations (voters!) in their fight for pure food and milk; and they took violators to court. There they testified to the unsanitary conditions and found themselves under cross-examination by defense lawyers. There were few convictions, no loss of licenses, and not much improvement in conditions. Finally, in 1915, the state pure food and drug commissioner appointed two WHPA members as deputy state food and drug inspectors. By then the public exposure, agitation, and public outcry were beginning to have effects.

Monthly reports at WHPA meetings showed improvements in markets and dairies. But the best news came when a delegation comprised of Dr. Heard, members of the WHPA, and the County Medical Society insisted on a hearing before the city commissioners. They presented their plan for a new ordinance with better enforcement. "Plainly displayed grading of milk," insisted Dr. Heard, and "all receptacles used by milk sellers [shall] be marked in classification of A, B and C, and . . . the city [shall] give wide publicity to the grades these letters stand for." Then, the delegation reasoned, "all dairies would strive to have their milk in the highest classification. . . ." The delegation went further and demanded tuberculosis-free cattle, to be guaranteed by regular veterinary tests, narrow-topped milk pails to prevent manure from falling in, the cooling of milk at the dairy before transport to market, screened bottling rooms, and use of a "reliable index for grading the sanitary conditions of the dairies" provided by the Bureau of Animal Industry, a component of the U.S. Department of Agriculture. The dairies put up a howl of protest, but backing by the Galveston Commercial Association, the Rotary Club, and the Galveston Labor Council convinced even reluctant city commissioners that public sentiment had swung in favor of regulation. They passed the ordinance. It had taken five years to get a modern system of milk protection for the city, and in the process WHPA members had become politically savvy. They had adopted traditional lobbying techniques, tried confrontational meetings, used muckraking tactics to report unsanitary conditions, published lists, called for boycotts, initiated lawsuits against offenders, legitimated their positions as inspectors through state appointments, and sought public support. In the process they learned an important lesson. By getting male voters to back them, they had made greater progress. Women knew they needed the vote. WHPA president Clara Ujffy said it best: "[W]ithout the ballot, [we] have little or nothing to say with regard to how such laws should be carried into effect. The day will come when we will have a voice, that's sure."

Working toward the right to vote stirred the imaginations of a number of Galveston reformers—many of whom had plunged into creating a new Galveston following the 1900 hurricane. Several attempts to form a long-lasting local suffrage society in the first decade of the twentieth century had failed. The city underwent dramatic physical changes with the sea wall construction and the grade raising. Life was extraordinarily difficult during those years, and the WHPA absorbed much of the energy of women reformers and directed it toward protecting public health and returning the city to its former beauty. But by 1912, timing was more propitious for founding a viable suffrage society.

In part this depended on the WHPA; suffragists usually came from the ranks of urban reformers and civic activists. As the WHPA began its second phase in 1912, focusing on the city's sanitation and public health problems, the organization moved from a conciliatory stance with city hall to a more confrontational one. By putting themselves into the political fracas but without the politi-

cal clout accorded voting men, WHPA members understood firsthand the weakness of "moral suasion" and "woman's influence." It is no coincidence that a movement entitling women to vote found a receptive audience among Galveston reformers. The WHPA had also taught women about open balloting and office holding in a democratic organization; they elected their own officers and divided into committees, giving women practical experience in how to respond to community needs—just as city commissioners were expected to do.

There were other causes for the woman suffrage movement's emergence in 1912. Better education, professional opportunities, and more women in the workforce helped them understand the conservative economic rationale that kept women voteless and lower paid. Minnie Fisher Cunningham, a graduate from the School of Pharmacy of the Medical Department of the University of Texas in Galveston and president of both the city and the state suffrage associations, asserted that when she took a job as prescription clerk at a Huntsville drugstore in 1901, she earned "$75 a month and everybody else $150. And now you could see what made a suffragette out of me—Equal Pay for Equal Work, only it wasn't equal work, I was the professional!" Galveston women reformers subscribed to national organizations that extolled the work of progressives. The General Federation of Women's Clubs featured women's civic responsibilities and encouraged them to take action and transform their cities and towns. The National American Woman Suffrage Association (NAWSA), headquartered in Washington, D.C., pelted local club women with pamphlets and fliers showing the connection between successful reform campaigns in states where women had the right to vote. The world was waking up to women's potential power and to women's unequal status.

Thus in February 1912, seventy-four white women and seven men took the plunge and signed a charter establishing the Galveston Equal Suffrage Association (GESA). Just when reformers were ready to launch this new suffrage society, there arrived a familiar catalyst from New York, Anna Maxwell Jones. She had come before in February 1901, when the city needed a women's civic league, and

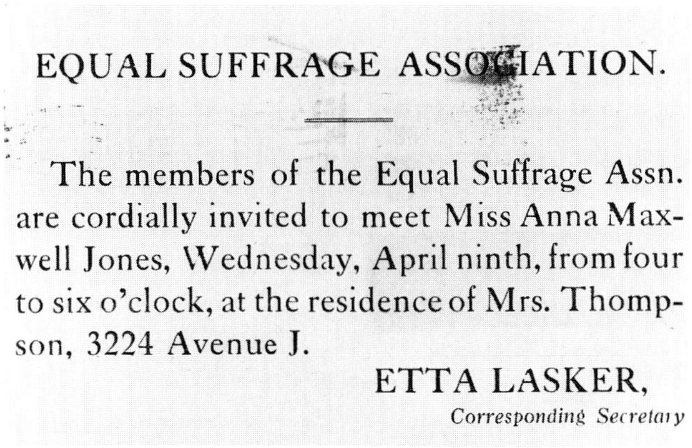

EQUAL SUFFRAGE ASSOCIATION.

The members of the Equal Suffrage Assn. are cordially invited to meet Miss Anna Maxwell Jones, Wednesday, April ninth, from four to six o'clock, at the residence of Mrs. Thompson, 3224 Avenue J.

ETTA LASKER,
Corresponding Secretary

FIGURE 4.11: Anna Maxwell Jones, former Galveston resident residing in New York, came in February 1912 to help start up a suffrage society in Galveston. She returned in April to greet the members of the successfully organized Galveston Equal Suffrage Association. (Courtesy Rosenberg Library, Galveston, Texas.)

she breathed life into the Women's Health Protective Association. Jones came again to her native state bearing the goodwill of NAWSA president Anna Howard Shaw. In her usual enthusiastic way, she organized a rally and brought the most important issues to the fore: women in six western states already had the vote, and so should Texas, she proclaimed, and leaders in the southeastern states were already mobilizing. Bringing the argument closer to home, she asserted that "as guardians of the home, protectors of the health of the family, intrusted [sic] with rearing and training of the children, we women are interested in the public welfare. . . . [T]he physical welfare and the moral uplift of the community [would] be more quickly brought about through the direct influence of the ballot in the hands of women." Others reminded listeners that women were "municipal housekeepers," and "in asking for the right to vote, they are following their housekeeping in the place where it is now being done, the polls." Issues such as equal pay for equal work and voting rights for every property owner were heard from the platform along with the underlying theme of citizenship. Nobody mentioned the

right of black women to vote, as white suffragists generally favored disfranchisement as a solution to the "race issue."

In the first year, the GESA invited no fewer than six suffrage speakers, including Anna Howard Shaw, to educate the city on the issues of woman suffrage. One young speaker, Perle Penfield, state suffrage fieldworker and Galveston medical student, praised the WHPA's reform efforts: "The present campaign being waged . . . here for pure milk has brought home to this woman the relation between disease and bad milk, and the necessity of control by enforced regulations. . . . The housewife . . . should have the responsibility and power of requiring enforcement of the laws. . . . she must become a voter." To recruit new members and strengthen its case, the GESA held teas; later GESA members became more bold and set up a booth at the Cotton Carnival and Exposition, leased space for a downtown headquarters, and presented a suffrage play. By 1913 membership had grown to 175 and by 1915 to 300, thirty-six of whom were men.

Statewide and national issues presented opportunities for the local suffragists: the Texas legislature put forth a married women's property rights bill, which GESA members endorsed. They stumped door to door gathering signatures on a petition to the Texas legislature for a state woman suffrage amendment. They worked tirelessly at educating voters: a subscription to NAWSA's *Woman's Journal* went to the public library; they persuaded the newspapers to offer articles on suffrage weekly; and they edited a "Suffrage Edition" that appeared in the Galveston *Tribune*. On May 2, 1914, while suffragists held simultaneous demonstrations all over the nation, GESA members publicly adopted a resolution asking Congress for a woman suffrage amendment. During the entire week preceding the day of celebration, GESA members had entertained and informed passersby along the Strand with a new gadget, the voiceless speech, wherein "large placards, in black and white, were turned slowly on easels . . . by members of the local suffragette organization," emphasizing in a dramatic way the limits on women's ability to participate in the body politic. Later that year, GESA president Minnie Fisher Cunningham "spoke for the right of women to vote from the back

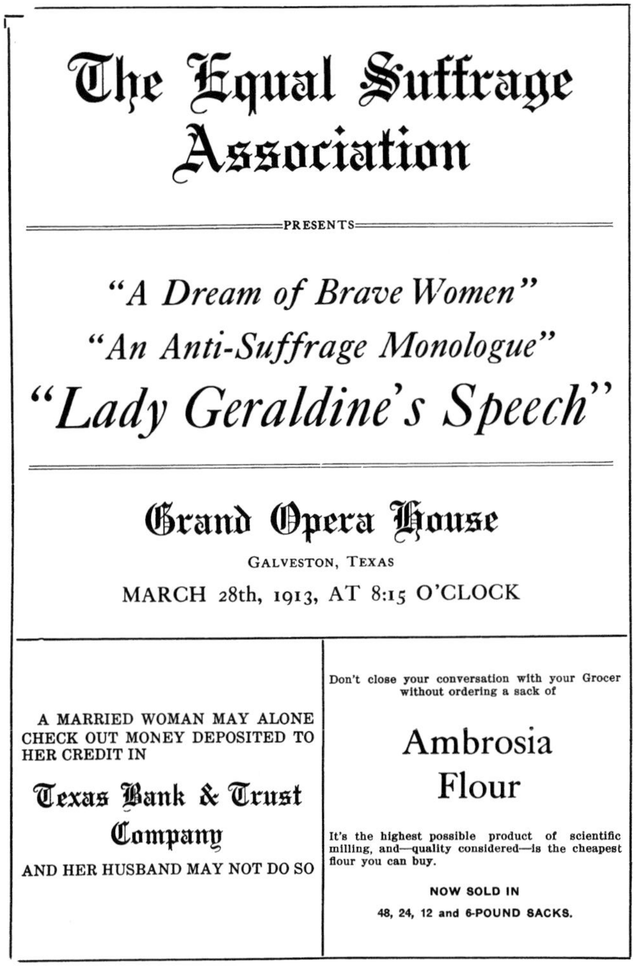

The Equal Suffrage Association

━━━ PRESENTS ━━━

"A Dream of Brave Women"

"An Anti-Suffrage Monologue"

"Lady Geraldine's Speech"

Grand Opera House

GALVESTON, TEXAS

MARCH 28th, 1913, AT 8:15 O'CLOCK

A MARRIED WOMAN MAY ALONE
CHECK OUT MONEY DEPOSITED TO
HER CREDIT IN

Texas Bank & Trust
Company

AND HER HUSBAND MAY NOT DO SO

Don't close your conversation with your Grocer
without ordering a sack of

Ambrosia
Flour

It's the highest possible product of scientific
milling, and—quality considered—is the cheapest
flour you can buy.

NOW SOLD IN

48, 24, 12 and 6-POUND SACKS.

FIGURE 4.12: To recruit new members and strengthen their case, Galveston suffragists and their daughters presented an evening's entertainment in the Grand Opera House, March 1913. The packed audience witnessed an antisuffragist monologue that pilloried the "antis," a tableau that portrayed famous women in history, and a suffrage comedy that called on the acting talents of seven prominent Galveston women. Membership in the Galveston Equal Suffrage Association grew from 175 to 300 in two years. (Courtesy Rosenberg Library, Galveston, Texas.)

seat of a touring car" in her first speech to the public. This was a daring act in 1914, and Minnie Fish, as her friends called her, was just the sort of person to do it first.

Minnie Fisher Cunningham was undoubtedly the most famous woman to emerge from Galveston between 1900 and 1915. Born in New Waverly, Texas, she moved to Galveston to become a pharmacy student at the Medical Department of the University of Texas in 1898. She survived the hurricane, met and married Beverly J. Cunningham, and worked a few years in Huntsville. The young couple returned to Galveston in 1907 just as the WHPA was making strides toward city revegetation. Cunningham was a suffragist long before most other Galveston women even thought about their own voting rights. She enthusiastically joined the GESA in 1912 and forged ahead to become its president in 1914. But as soon as she took the position, she found herself defending the concept of woman suffrage not just with men voters but with Texas club women meeting in the state convention in Galveston. The Texas Federation of Women's Clubs (TFWC) would not allow on their agenda any discussion of the right to vote, and Galveston's Wednesday Club, a reading and book study club to which Cunningham belonged, refused to allow the GESA any part in the entertainment of the TFWC. This made Cunningham mad. "I feel black and blue all over about that business. I feel so culpable in allowing myself to be bound to silence on such an important subject. . . . I can't help regretting that I didn't make a 'scene!'" It would be only a matter of time before the TFWC endorsed woman suffrage, but by then Cunningham had left them in the dust to pursue her goals at the state level.

Cunningham was so far ahead of her peers that she became restless even with members of the GESA. For example, she urged the local chapter to put some money into maintaining a headquarters at the beach, where hundreds of tourists played. She wrote state suffrage president Annette Finnigan in 1914:

The darling hope of my heart for three years has been a beach headquarters in the summer, and open air speaking on excursion days.

It seems to me we are letting a glorious opportunity to reach all Texas slip right through our fingers. . . . Last year we had money in the bank which we had made for the express purpose of establishing a headquarters, and because the price was high we kept our money in the bank. . . . I wish you could come down . . . and see the potential readers of Suffrage literature and listeners to Suffrage speeches wandering up and down the Boulevard with nothing to do.

A second time she urged GESA members to open a beach headquarters but without success. They chose instead to open a booth for a week at the Cotton Carnival and Exposition in August but with no speeches on Sunday "on account of a few very strict Sabbath keepers" in the GESA. Extremely unhappy with the traditionalism of even the most progressive women in Galveston, she longed to move on to a bigger job. In 1915 she was reelected as GESA president. She wrote to Finnigan, "The Galveston organization at its annual meeting Saturday did me the honor of returning me to office for another year. In spite of my stern determination not to be returned. It makes me feel like a 'spell' of sickness to think of another year, but please don't tell on me." Before long she got her wish to move on. Annette Finnigan stepped down and Cunningham won the Texas Equal Suffrage Association (TESA) presidency, a position she held until passage of the Susan B. Anthony Amendment in 1920. Cunningham's energy, political savvy, and innovation in recruiting Texas legislators to the cause—techniques she learned in Galveston—brought Texas into the national limelight as one of the few southern states in 1918 to allow women to vote in the state primary and as the first southern state of four to ratify the amendment in 1919. When the Tennessee legislature finally cast the deciding ballots in 1920, women in the United States had gained the right to vote.

There is no doubt that the efforts of local suffragists in Galveston added to the state's success. The fund raisers, speakers, booths, canvasses for petitions, and rallies all added strength to a movement for women's rights. Progressive women were more fully politicized by 1915; the WHPA campaign for a safer, more sanitary

FIGURE 4.13: Minnie Fisher Cunningham, president of the Galveston Equal Suffrage Association from 1914 to 1915 and of the Texas Equal Suffrage Association from 1915 to 1920, was undoubtedly the most famous woman to emerge from Galveston between 1900 and 1915. (Courtesy Austin History Center, Austin Public Library, E.4 B.7 [3].)

life in Galveston had taught them political lessons, and they practiced pressure group policy making with intelligence and success. The logical leap to the suffrage movement prepared women to become voters. Because it had not been a birthright for them, because it took years of hard struggle to convince men that women should vote, the victory was all the sweeter. After that, few Galveston women could take this particular act of citizenship casually.

For African Americans, Progressive Era initiatives that emerged in Galveston in the wake of the hurricane of 1900 had a completely different meaning. For whites it meant cleaning up city government with a city commission plan; putting thousands of dollars into restoring wharves, railroad terminals, silos, grain elevators, and a causeway; restructuring cotton compress factories; reopening the Strand's "emporium"; bringing new business prospects to the city; beautifying and sanitizing the city; mobilizing women for the vote; and constructing the city's defenses against future storms. African Americans could certainly feel pride and hope for the future in the city's reemergence like a phoenix from the ashes. But as Galveston remade itself, its white citizens, now fully in control of governmental authority, assumed a patronizing attitude toward African Americans, eliminated them from political participation, and denied them equal access to public facilities. Ironically, as blacks were excluded from political policy making, white women found themselves included. As seen in the days immediately after the storm, Galveston newspapers and profit-hungry authors made black men seem unworthy of assuming public responsibilities, while white women were praised for their selfless sacrifices, especially through the Red Cross. Of course, blacks also sacrificed for victims of the storm, but public approval was rare. A sea change had come to Galveston: white middle- and upper-class women, although not yet voters, found themselves cooperating with and then successfully confronting city commissioners. In effect they replaced black aldermen—not literally, of course, but in their abilities to make public policy proposals outside the formal governing structure. The result was a rise in white female power at the expense of black men.

City commissioners were elected by city residents at large, which, because of demographics, made it impossible for blacks to be represented on the city's highest governing body. With Galveston's black population only 22 percent of the total, it would have taken a miracle for a black man to win election to the city commission. Thus, African Americans had no authoritative voice in decisions regarding their welfare. And, unlike white women, who had the WHPA, they had no effective single lobbying group to take their agenda and their interests to city hall. The consequence of the storm and municipal restructuring, therefore, affected the black community differently and more negatively. Yet, this does not mean that Galveston African Americans were impossibly downtrodden. In fact, blacks proudly pointed to a rather substantial economic base in 1909; they took pride in their three schools; and they maintained their solidarity through their schools, churches, benevolent associations, clubs, bands, and business and educational organizations. The year after the city commission plan took effect, politicians in Austin struck another blow at African Americans: they voted to adopt the Alexander W. Terrell Amendment to the state constitution, which made voters pay an annual $1.50 poll tax for the right to vote. For many, both white and black, this amount was beyond their means, and thus poor people in all parts of the state were effectively disfranchised. These measures were followed in the 1920s by white-only primaries, and blacks were eliminated from voting in the party primaries, where the most important candidate decisions were made, particularly in the solidly Democratic South. For those blacks who could afford the poll tax and who attempted to vote, there was always the danger of violence from outraged whites. It was no wonder that black voting in Texas declined from a high of one hundred thousand voters in the 1890s to five thousand in 1906: the law was 95 percent effective and 100 percent undemocratic.

Editor William H. Noble vented his anger in the pages of the Galveston *City Times*: "The colored voter cannot afford to lose any strength; the *Times* has at all times been opposed to restrictions on manhood suffrage . . . [but] while the law is in force . . . go and pay your poll tax and arm yourself with a weapon." But the poll tax did its work: out of 4,000 (17 percent) eligible black county voters, 675 were able to pay the tax; 500 Galveston blacks could vote in a city of 36,000.

With so few black voters, the Texas legislature continued to restrict black rights. The low point in race relations came between 1904 and 1907 when the Adjutant General of Texas claimed that blacks were no longer interested in the state militia. He disbanded the "colored battalion of the State Guard" and required all black militias to cease and return all state property to Austin. The meaning behind this was clear; blacks were no longer considered worthy of assuming military obligations for the state. The Galveston Hawley Guards, which had played a largely ceremonial role in city parades and celebrations, lost a significant symbol of citizenship and the freedom to bear arms in a state militia. It was a constitutional right taken from them. William Noble wrote angrily that "where the colored citizens have the voice of voting an honest man's ballot without the interference of unjust state restrictions, he is respected as an American citizen. . . . do you think for a moment that in Illinois, the Adjutant General would order the colored troops disbanded as in Texas, Georgia and elsewhere?"

The Republican party of Texas, the party of Abraham Lincoln and emancipation, turned a deaf ear to African American protests. Thus separation of the races continued. City after city segregated streetcars, one of the last remaining public places where whites and blacks sat together. Schools, churches, auditoriums, parks, trains, hotels, restaurants, drinking fountains, and restrooms were already segregated. The only remaining places where whites and blacks had much contact were in homes, where blacks worked as servants for white families, and on the docks, where longshoremen and screwmen labored through separate unions.

A white citizen drive to segregate Galveston's streetcars began in 1905, the year Houston adopted the ordinance. W. H. Bearden, editor of the black-owned *New Idea*, railed against the Galveston *Tribune* for advocating Jim Crow streetcars and labeled it a "poor white newspaper" that "represent[s] the destructive elements of the community." But the petition to adopt segregated trolley cars went before the city commissioners. *City Times* editor William Noble appeared before them with this argument: "I do not think it is right to discriminate against a people when they have not shown cause . . . it is only a matter of plain prejudice against the colored people." To their credit, Commissioners Isaac Kempner and Herman C. Lange voted against the law. This was unusual, for in most southern cities, government officials voted unanimously for the segregation of streetcars. Kempner argued: "I know of no concrete case that has been called to the attention of this board where there has been difficulty on the street cars which would justify or warrant us passing this measure." And he lambasted the other three commissioners for the humiliation that it would cause blacks. In his concluding statements, Mayor Henry Landes weakly defended this vote for segregation. "Well gentlemen, I regret very much that this question was ever brought up. We have a better class of colored people in Galveston in the way of deportment, character and civic duty than any other city in Texas or in the South, I believe. . . . there has been very little necessity for such an ordinance, but inasmuch as the matter has been brought up and discussed at such length, I believe that it is best for both parties under the circumstances, to adopt the ordinance." Galveston lawyer Joseph Cuney immediately responded with a vehement protest that ran in the *City Times* and in the Galveston *Daily News*, but the results were the same. In fact, discrimination intensified. In 1907, when 190 black citizens petitioned to build a bathhouse at 37th Street and the sea wall, whites prevented it. So while whites enjoyed bathhouses along the sea wall, African Americans had none.

For the black community, increasing prejudice and the hard heartedness of whites presented a struggle for survival, but black Galvestonians rose to the challenge and, insulated as they were forced to be, established a resilient and energetic community. When their civil rights were severely abrogated, they defended themselves with eloquence and logic. Instead of mourning these events, they created public celebrations for life and freedom in Juneteeth festivities, Labor Day parades, and summer fests for children and the elderly. They did this through their own clubs and societies, business leagues, and charitable institutions. Churches, Sunday schools, and church-sponsored activities for young people kept alive self-esteem and faith. African Americans fostered a love of learning and used their schools as cultural centers for the education of children and adults. Just at a time when race relations seemed to have reached a low point, the African American community found itself expanding economically. Its city population reached nearly ten thousand in 1909, and the *City Times* estimated its annual income in salaries at $332,514. Over one thousand black men were regularly employed at the wharves; four physicians, including Dr. Mary Moore, founder of the Hubbard Clinic, and four lawyers had set up practice, not to mention twenty-three teachers and administrators, and sixteen clergymen. Seventy-five black-owned businesses representing thirty-seven different occupations and professions served the community. The idea that African Americans would not work unless forced, a notion expressed at the height of the post-storm panic, proved to be just another racist stereotype.

If any institutions should be credited with fostering an aura of independence and self-sufficiency, they were churches and schools. Scholars of African American history have recorded that black churches were more than houses of worship; they served as forums for debate and sources of education and economic cooperation. They offered a place to air grievances, to raise money for projects, and to train leaders. Although the hurricane destroyed every one of the fourteen black churches in Galveston, by 1910 fifteen churches stood in full operation. Sunday schools taught children moral principles, racial pride, and Christian faith: they gave children positive experiences. Church picnics to Dickinson on the mainland "with swings, dance floors, . . . shade trees, . . . everything a person would want for recreation" provided freedom for children and adults alike from the reminders of Jim Crow laws. Churches hosted visiting associations—the Colored Masons of Texas, state denominational conferences, Baptist Young People's conventions, the Epworth League, the Afro-American Council, and the National Negro Business League. When injustice rolled over Galveston African Americans in waves, religious sanctuaries turned into halls filled with righteous anger. The Ministers' Council meeting at St. Augustine Episcopal Church in 1906 condemned the lynching of a Louisiana man. Wesley Tabernacle Church members in 1914 began what they claimed was "the first Anti-lynching Society ever to be organized in the South. . . ." Avenue L Baptist Church hosted the first local meeting of the National Association for the Advancement of Colored People. Self-reliance and positive, even radical, approaches to life, were the common ground found in black churches, healing places for the wounds of intolerance.

Schools offered another avenue for black achievement. In 1885 Galveston chartered Central Public (High) for black children from grades six through eight. In 1888 school trustees hired John R. Gibson from Ohio, a graduate of Wilberforce University, as principal of Central High. He continued in that position until 1936. Clara Barton named Gibson head of the Red Cross Auxiliary for Galveston African Americans in 1900, and he served for twenty years as consul for Liberia after his appointment by President William McKinley in 1901. A distinguished educator and an outstanding community leader, Gibson made sure that Central High School would not be neglected. In 1893 the school board hired architect Nicholas Clayton to design a two-story stone school building at 26th Street and Avenue M for about thirteen thousand dollars, one of the finest black high schools in the South. It suffered extensive damage in the 1900 storm, and underwent "raising" in 1909 at a cost of $2,700. But even before that, Central High School had become the intellectual and cultural center of the black community, offering musical concerts, lectures, alumni reunions, and elaborate graduation ceremonies. Mothers' Clubs raised money for extracurricular excursions and materials, and after 1905, not without controversy, Central High became the site of the only black public library in Texas.

FIGURE 4.14: Avenue L Baptist Church in 1917. African American churches fostered independence and self-sufficiency, and served as forums for debate and sources of education and economic cooperation. They offered a place to air grievances, to raise money for projects, and to train leaders. Although the hurricane destroyed every one of the fourteen black churches, by 1910 fifteen churches stood in full operation. (Courtesy Rosenberg Library, Galveston, Texas.)

FIGURE 4.15: Central High School students, a teacher, and the principal, John R. Gibson, in 1917. Gibson, a graduate of Wilberforce University, continued as principal until 1936. Clara Barton named him head of the Red Cross Auxiliary for Galveston African Americans in 1900, and he served for twenty years as consul for Liberia after his appointment by President William McKinley in 1901. Central High suffered damage in the 1900 Storm but was restored to resume its position as intellectual and cultural center of the black community, offering musical concerts, lectures, alumni reunions, and elaborate graduation ceremonies. (Courtesy Rosenberg Library, Galveston, Texas.)

In 1904, the city celebrated the opening of the Rosenberg Library, the gift of Henry Rosenberg, a Swiss immigrant who had made Galveston his home in 1843. He turned merchandising and banking into a personal fortune, and when he died in 1893 gave the majority of his estate to the city. He willed four hundred thousand dollars to be set aside to provide a public library. The opening of the library stood as a centerpiece in Galveston's recovery. But the question arose, should African Americans be allowed to use the Rosenberg Library? His will intended a public library for all Galveston citizens; to deny blacks usage of the library would violate Rosenberg's bequest. One of the fears articulated by the board of trustees was that African Americans' desire to use the library might be an expression of a larger ambition—seeking "social equality." The state legislature then passed a bill creating a "Colored Branch of Rosenberg Library" as an annex to Central High School. Editor William Noble opposed the creation of a branch library and wrote, "No white person . . . need have any fear of the Negro seeking social equality because of being admitted to a library built of fine stone. . . . The negro is not seeking social equality; he does not care for it, but he does insist upon being treated as an American citizen in all manner due him. . . ." Noble's point was once again to condemn segregation and its pernicious spread over the community.

Overall, however, the black community welcomed the branch because the alternative was no support at all from the Rosenberg Library Association—and thus no library for the black community. W. H. Bearden of the *New Idea* intoned that "any Negro who refuses to encourage the colored library given out of the Rosenberg fund is either a fool or an ignoramus. . . . they are blocking their race's progress and standing in the way of their own intellectual light. . . . it is evident [Rosenberg] intended the Library to be a separate institution. Besides it costs the race nothing." In the first year after its opening, the "Colored Branch" stocked 1,100 volumes and twenty-one periodicals. Leon Morgan, principal of Central High after 1941, remembered that at the time, this "meant that Central had a better library than [all white] Ball High."

FIGURE 4.16: In 1904, the city celebrated the opening of the Rosenberg Library, the gift of Henry Rosenberg, a Swiss immigrant who had made Galveston his home in 1843. Questions arose over the use of the library by black patrons. (Courtesy Rosenberg Library, Galveston, Texas.)

The library was a definite boon for students, and the high school continued to produce graduates despite an unsuccessful attempt in 1904 by city government to close it. Between 1891 and 1914, Central High graduated 121 students, two thirds of whom were young women. In 1912 Central High opened a night school for adolescents and adults, with private donations paying for the instruction. Sixty-five students ranging in age from fourteen to fifty-four attended and made good use of the building. Eventually the black community on its own raised funds for a neighborhood playground. Today Central High continues to serve the community as the Old Central Cultural Center, a museum and resource center for African American life and history.

Community celebrations also brought a sense of solidarity to Galveston African Americans. Historians claim that parades and public community festivals provided groups who were considered to be on the outside, or marginalized, an opportunity to enter public life, to proclaim their presence, and to present an oppositional point of view to the dominant culture. Parades could bring with them a confrontational edge, such as when blacks in 1905 celebrated Independence Day, while white southerners, reminded of Confederate defeat, held no Fourth of July festivities. National symbols and holidays imbued with African American themes testify to the richness and ebullience of a continually evolving culture.

Labor Day celebrations honored the integrity of black labor and labor unions. In 1903, 1,500 cotton jammers, teamsters, Mallory line freight haulers, railroad men, Hawley Guards, Holloman's Juvenile Light Guards, the drum corps, the Island City brass band, and the Women's Nineteenth of June Committee paraded through the streets to the Gulf City Park. Later that night they ended their celebration at the Sea Wall Pavilion, "the best pleasure resort in town for colored people." And every year the *City Times* and the *New Idea* presented the August Children's Day Parade and Summer Night Festival at the Sea Wall Pavilion (also known as Children's and Old Folks' Day).

The plan for the summer festival began with William H. Noble, editor of the *City Times*, the first black newspaper in Galveston. Educated at the University of Chicago, Noble wanted to offer a joyful celebration to Galveston blacks supported by both black and white businessmen. Through his editorials he opposed segregation and discrimination at every turn, but the Summer Night Festival was his way of endorsing the black community with the gift of laughter. The festival featured parades as well as literary, athletic, and musical contests, which offered special hope to young people. It also brought relief to workers in the hottest month of the year and invited older and younger people to get to know and appreciate each other.

Of all the national holidays, festivals, parades, and gatherings, the greatest celebration and perhaps the one that meant the most to black Texans was Juneteenth, which commemorated June 19, 1865. On that day Texas slaves first heard General Order No. 3, declaring their emancipation, delivered in Galveston by Union Major General Gordon Granger. By 1900 the parade and the program were organized entirely by the Women's Nineteenth of June Committee, and the program always addressed issues of black equality—contemporary and historical. Both men and women rode in parade carriages and made speeches, but it was young women who took center stage—one dressed in the costume of the goddess of liberty, another reading the Emancipation Proclamation. Liberty's statue represents for this nation freedom, but the face of liberty is a face of stone without race or nationality. Black women understood the power of the symbol of freedom in a feminine embodiment, transformed it, and applied it to suit their own situation—their hope for freedom of opportunity for themselves and for their children. Juneteenth celebrations were filled with allegorical meaning and reminded black Texans that freedom in any age is worth the struggle.

In the final analysis, Galveston African Americans made a commitment to take care of their own the best way they could. Because health care and care of orphans and the aged were areas that fell under segregation laws, it was in large part up to the black community to provide for those groups. Beginning in 1901, with Clara Barton's

FIGURE 4.17: William H. Noble was editor of the *City Times*, the first black newspaper in Galveston. Educated at the University of Chicago, Noble wanted to offer a joyful celebration to Galveston blacks supported by both black and white businessmen. Through his editorials he had opposed segregation at every turn since 1900; the Summer Night Festival was his way of celebrating with the black community the gift of laughter. (Courtesy Rosenberg Library, Galveston, Texas.)

contribution to the African American Red Cross Auxiliary, John R. Gibson and twenty-six others chartered the Galveston Relief Association to raise money to build a Home for Indigent Colored People, which was actually a home for the aged. The need for such a home was made all too clear in the hurricane's aftermath, when elderly blacks were found huddled in the ruins of churches and city and federal buildings. Magnolia Sealy had brought this to the attention of Clara Barton, who initiated the contact with Gibson. The Galveston Relief Association, guided by an executive committee comprised of black school principals, Gibson, H. T. Davis, and W. N. Cummings, bought ten acres of land in La Marque, where "the soil is rich enough, by proper management, to make the Home almost self-supporting." By 1912, the association was equipped to begin the construction of a cottage for the aged.

Hospital care for Galveston blacks had traditionally been rendered by the Old City Hospital, but in 1902 federal, state, and private funds contributed to the opening of Negro Hospital, a separate building for African Americans staffed by black doctors and nurses. Initially, the wing lacked equipment, bedding, hospital gowns, and amusements for the patients; the situation was ameliorated somewhat when John R. Gibson raised $450 for hospital beds. His example was followed by the founding of the Colored Women's Hospital Aid Society, which from 1909 until the 1960s, when segregation ended, provided essential equipment as well as special favors for the patients and staff. The Hospital Aid Society affiliated with the National Association of Colored Women, an overarching body of club women that by 1914 was fifty thousand strong with over a thousand clubs. Middle-class Galveston women benefited from this national affiliation, tapping into literature, progressive concepts of civic responsibility, and programs for social and racial "uplift," but the Hospital Aid Society's most important contribution to the black community came in countering the damaging effects of segregation.

For Galveston's African Americans, the legacy of the storm brought a revival in church and school rebuilding along with related societies, clubs, businesses, cultural self-help groups, and community celebrations. Cut off politically, black editors and individuals protested the needless extension of segregation and formed organizations to counter racist laws. In 1908 potential voters organized a poll-tax club "for the purpose of getting an interest among the colored citizens to qualify for the necessary political standing in the city . . .," and at the height of the suffrage movement Galveston black women formed the Negro Women Voters' League of Galveston. Thus Galveston African Americans survived and thrived as a community within a community, while adding valuable economic and cultural components to the post-storm recovery.

The sea wall and grade raising were tested periodically during this time. A hurricane in 1909 caused some scouring and deterioration of the sea wall and necessitated repairs and modifications recommended by General Henry M. Robert. But the greatest test of both efforts came on August 17, 1915, when a storm comparable to the 1900 hurricane hit the island. The storm passed just south of Galveston, and while the barometric readings remained higher than those taken in 1900 (28.63 inches versus 28.42), the tide was half a foot higher. The highest windspeed was 93 mph at 2:37 A.M. on August 17, and hurricane force winds continued on the island for 19 hours. The highest wind speed documented in 1900 was 84 mph, but the anemometer blew away; officials estimated that winds reached 120 mph before the end of the storm. Meteorologists in 1915 calculated that the storms "were of about equal intensity." Results of the storm, fortunately, were not.

"Great Hurricane Sweeps Texas Coast; Galveston Seawall Again Paramount," read the headline in the *Daily News* on August 17. "Subjected to a test that could hardly have been more terrific, the great Galveston seawall again was tried and found not wanting. Against the battering of giant seas it stood stanchly [sic] throughout every foot of its five miles." "The sea-wall at Galveston, Tex., was the city's salvation during the hurricane of Aug. 16–17. This is the outstanding feature, from the engineering viewpoint, of the effect of the recent storm," reported the *Engineering Record. Engineering News* was no less convinced. "Thanks to the precautions in the way of seawall and grade elevation taken subsequent to the disastrous storm of 1900, the loss of life and damage to property was comparatively small in the city. . . ." The *Engineering News* correspondent, R. P. Babbitt, was even more congratulatory: "Had it not been for the seawall there would now be only a heap of ruins to mark the site of this great Texas seaport. This magnificent wall, extending . . . along the Gulf front of the city, was impregnable to the fury of the waves which beat against it but were baffled at every point." All of this tribute notwithstanding, portions of the wall were undermined, its concrete sidewalk seriously damaged, and areas of backfilling washed away. The greatest storm damage befell the approaches to the causeway connecting Galveston to the mainland.

The storm washed away the earthen roadbed leading to the 2,455 feet of reinforced concrete viaduct and destroyed the pipe carrying the city's water supply from the mainland. But the loss of life and property experienced in 1900 was not repeated; in Galveston eight were killed while elsewhere 304 died. With such proof of the wall's strength, urban engineers and planners might be forgiven a little self-satisfaction.

Amid the chaos in the wake of the Galveston storm of Aug. 17 one structure stands out in bolt [sic] relief, a monument to engineering skill and foresight—the seawall. . . . Galveston's seawall was the city's salvation, and to the engineers who designed it and to the contractors who built it the Texas town owes a debt of gratitude which can never be adequately repaid. . . . It takes a catastrophe like the Galveston storm to demonstrate to a public, often forgetful of those to whom it owes its safety, that the civil engineer is the foundationstone upon which the physical welfare of cities must be built. . . . City officials . . . may well ponder over the Galveston lesson and take inventory of their own state of preparedness against unforeseen catastrophes which engineers can aid them in preventing.

FIGURE 4.18: In the aftermath of the 1915 storm, the causeway to the main-land stood unharmed, but the earthen approaches to it and the water lines under it were damaged. (Courtesy Rosenberg Library, Galveston, Texas.)

FIGURE 4.19: Following the storm of August 7, 1915, Galvestonians discovered the efficacy of the sea wall in saving the city from utter destruction. Although Sea Wall Boulevard was reduced to rubble, and houses near the Gulf were damaged, the sea wall stood, a formidable structure between land and sea. (Fort Crockett repairs and restorations, 1916; Folder 060, RG 077, National Archives Southwest Region, Fort Worth, Texas.)

FIGURE 4.20: The sea wall was and is still today a monument to engineering skill and citizen fortitude. (Courtesy Rosenberg Library, Galveston, Texas.)

Citizens felt secure enough after the storm to send a telegram to the Associated Press refusing any form of relief and expressing their profound thanks "in this triumphant battle with the elements that similar assistance [as that offered in 1900] is unnecessary." They went on to "assure friends and admirers everywhere of this sincere pledge to strive diligently and heartily to attain that superior success which last night's victory promises for the community." The sea wall, a visible and formidable construction separating land and sea, received the bulk of the credit for preserving the city. The grade raising, largely completed and invisible by 1915, was no less a factor in the city's survival.

After 1915 the city could relax somewhat, at least with regard to hurricanes. The sea wall and grade raising were successful; buildings, property, and human lives would never be threatened as they had been in 1900. The causeway offered exit to those who would take it; rebuilt structures provided shelter and safety to those who would not. But the island residents were not the same, literally and figuratively. Galveston's population had recovered—surprisingly—and the 1910 census counted only 808 fewer inhabitants than in 1900. In the fifteen years after the storm, major changes transformed the island—not simply normal growth or development expected with the passage of time—but dramatic shifts in the political, social, racial, and gendered realms of the city, shifts that were shaped by the events of September 8, 1900.

CONCLUSION

"I will never forget those days"

It was the late part of November, and I had done so much burning

and so much work that I just gave out. I was sick for a long time.

I can still smell the dead, and the burning bodies, like burnt

sugar. I will never forget those days. I roamed around for sixty-one

years after that, never able to sit down. . . . That old hurricane

didn't even have a name, but she packed a mighty punch.

P. G. TIPP

NO ONE CAN KNOW what Galveston would be like had the 1900 Storm not occurred; there is no "control" community with which to compare the "test" community. The hurricane became the city's defining event, in many ways its creation myth. Island residents bisected their lives into "before the storm" and "after the storm" components, and, even in the 1990s, the event remains "The Storm."

Like the proverbial rock thrown into a pond, the September hurricane generated ripples far beyond its point of impact. The size of the disaster in terms of death and property destruction was staggering for the time. Immediate public health concerns—body disposal, fresh water needs, food, medical care, housing—demanded an unprecedented level of organized response. And that response laid the foundation for and unquestionably shaped the city that rose from the rubble.

Once the most pressing needs of the survivors had been addressed, the sheer magnitude of the devastation—the almost complete destruction of all aspects of urban infrastructure—gave leaders an opportunity to rebuild in a thoughtful, intentional way. The coincidence of reconstruction with progressive reform movements made Galveston a laboratory of sorts, a testing ground for new ideas about government, society, and technology.

Politically, the city opted for change. For a variety of reasons, some real and some imagined, Galvestonians freely abandoned a democratic electoral process for promised gains in administrative efficiency. Improved local administration, in turn, opened the

FIGURE CONCL.I: Certificates like this were sold to grieving families and friends after the storm. For those who did not have any bodies to bury or graves to tend, such a certificate might be the only remembrance. Death counts for the hurricane varied widely, ranging as high as twelve thousand. The accepted figure, and the one used in this work, is six thousand. When deaths on the mainland are added, the toll reaches approximately ten thousand. (Courtesy of the author.)

doors to financial investments in the city's recovery that propelled Galveston back into the regional and national economy.

Technologically, the island responded to the physical assault of the hurricane with unwavering faith in engineering methods, professional engineers, and an astonishing level of environmental hubris. Unconcerned with the possible long-term ramifications of massive civil engineering intervention, the city, county, state, and federal governments embarked upon a construction program that literally remade the island—a concrete sea wall and the raising of the land. The Gulf Coast barrier island, a narrow strip of sand that shifted and moved according to tides and storms, was monumentally reinforced against future attacks.

The social consequences of the storm and its recovery were probably the least expected and most unintended. News of the hurricane brought many national organizations to the rescue, and the Red Cross was among the most important of these for the way it modeled a new role for urban women activists. Galveston's women, already skilled at providing charity within the community, assumed leadership positions in the relief effort. These official positions—public acknowledgement of the ability and propriety of women working on a civic stage—created a new set of political actors for Galveston. Experience gained in administering disaster relief was put to use in revegetation programs, public health issues, and finally, woman suffrage.

Women's political success, however, came after black men had been removed, for the most part, from local politics. For African Americans, the storm hastened and legitimized the imposition of Jim Crow measures in the city. Despite individual stories of sacrifice and heroism, descriptions of black behavior during and after the disaster overwhelmingly conveyed a criminal or infantile impression. Black citizens were often coerced into especially odious work clearing bodies and wreckage, and they legitimately complained of unequal distribution of relief supplies. Changing the city's form of government further limited black representation and input into city policies. Passage of a poll tax by the state legislature—common practice throughout the South—resulted in a dras-

FIGURE CONCL.2: While those familiar with the history of the 1900 Storm realize that the disaster was a hurricane, many know the event as the "Galveston Flood." This may be attributable in part to a lack of understanding about storm surges and tides during a hurricane and the fact that several of the country's newspapers referred to the tragedy as a "flood." That the event entered the national consciousness is evidenced by this picture of a ride at the Coney Island amusement park in New York, taken sometime between 1901 and 1906. (Detroit Publishing Company Photograph Collection, courtesy Prints and Photographs Division, Library of Congress, Washington, D.C.)

tic decline in voting by black citizens and even more actions to limit the civil rights of black Texans. During this time, states were consolidating Jim Crow throughout the South, and if Galvestonians could be convinced that blacks were childlike, criminal, or incompetent, passage of such measures would be that much easier.

The black community reacted by protesting and by developing its own strong economic and social realm. African American doctors, educators, clergy, journalists, and other professionals protested moves to assure white supremacy at the same time that they created their own civic life. Churches and schools anchored this community within a community, and black Galvestonians thrived despite the institutionalized discrimination of the time.

Given subsequent events, a strong case may be made that Galveston's stock was in decline even before the September catastrophe. The evolving rail and water transportation network ultimately favored Houston, Galveston's hated northern rival, and critics charged that the Galveston Wharf Company was ill-equipped to compete in the rapidly changing marketplace. In *Against the Tide*, Cornelia Dean writes that "Galveston had made a Faustian bargain, and it would pay the price. Bad weather, bad luck, bad timing, and the decision to bet everything on a seawall had put the city on a long, downhill slide." But it was really more com-

plicated than that. The city bet on far more than simply a sea wall, and other forces were working against it in regional economics.

After September 1900, competitors emphasized the ongoing threat of hurricane devastation, and the discovery of oil at Spindletop a mere four months after the storm was an additional blow to the city's economic future. Geographic realities worked against the island—there was simply not enough space along its already cramped waterfront for all of the services expected in a modern port, especially one handling petroleum products. Acres and acres of tank farms and refineries settled in along the Houston ship channel and on the shores of rivers and bayous around Beaumont, Port Arthur, and Orange. As the feasibility of dredging deep water channels dramatically increased, Galveston's natural harbor lost its value.

But this is hindsight. After the 1900 Storm, Galveston did not see itself as out of the race. The city took immediate, aggressive steps to relieve, recover, restore, and regain position and status in the state. Realizing the stakes were high, city leaders took advantage of an almost literally clean slate to remake Galveston as a progressive southern city. To examine the hurricane of 1900 as only an extremely dramatic weather event is to miss its true significance. The catastrophe of September 8, 1900, was also a catalyst for change, a source of political, social—even topographical—transformation that was undertaken to save this unique city on a sandbar.

BIBLIOGRAPHICAL ESSAY

BECAUSE THIS WORK was written for a more popular, general audience, it lacks the full scholarly apparatus of footnotes, endnotes, or bibliography. Nevertheless, we realize the debts that we owe to those laboring in the same trenches. Additionally, some readers may be curious about particular items or want more information. While this work is built upon other more general histories of Texas, Progressivism, African Americans, women, the environment, and technology, what follows is not a detailed accounting of sources, but rather a listing of material most closely concerned with Galveston, the storm, and the particular issues addressed in this book.

GENERAL

A number of sources were used throughout this book. Any work on Galveston, as mentioned elsewhere, must begin with David G. McComb, *Galveston: A History* (Austin: University of Texas Press, 1986). Other more general histories exist, but McComb's work is the most completely documented, and Earl W. Fornell, *The Galveston Era: The Texas Crescent on the Eve of Secession* (Austin: University of Texas Press, 1961) is a detailed history of the city before the Civil War. Lynn M. Alperin, *Custodians of the Coast: History of the United States Army Corps of Engineers at Galveston* (Galveston: U.S. Army Corps of Engineers, 1977), is extremely useful for its recounting of the island's ongoing negotiation with the Gulf of Mexico and engineering efforts to stabilize the port and the island. The two major books on the 1900 Storm, John Edward Weems, *A Weekend in September* (College Station: Texas A&M University Press, 1957, 1980) and Herbert Molloy Mason Jr., *Death from the Sea* (New York: Dial Press, 1972), both contain brief descriptions of life before the storm. Other background information was obtained from Elizabeth Hayes Turner, *Women, Culture, and Community: Religion and Reform in Galveston, 1880–1920* (New York: Oxford University Press, 1997); Patricia Bellis Bixel, "Working the Waterfront on Film: Commercial Photography and Community Studies" (Ph.D. dissertation, Rice University, Houston, 1997); and Stephen P. Kretzmann, "A House Built Upon the Sand: Race, Class, Gender, and the Galveston Hurricane of 1900" (Ph.D. dissertation, University of Wisconsin, Madison, 1995). We also used material from Galveston newspapers from the period—the *Daily News, Tribune, New Idea, Journal,* and *City Times* (all available in at least partial runs on microfilm).

INTRODUCTION

Francis Sheridan's full account of his visit to Galveston may be found in Willis W. Pratt, ed., *Galveston Island: The Journal of Francis C. Sheridan, 1839–1840* (Austin: University of Texas Press, 1954). There are many wonderful works that discuss Galveston's historic architecture, among them, Ellen Beasley and Stephen Fox, *Galveston Architecture Guidebook* (Houston: Rice University Press, 1996); Ellen Beasley, *The Alleys and Back Buildings of Galveston* (Houston: Rice University Press, 1996); and Stephen Fox, "Broadway: Galveston, Texas," in Jan Cigliano and Sarah Bradford Landau, eds., *The Grand American Avenue, 1850–1920* (San Francisco: Pomegranate Artbooks, 1994), 206–229. For Galveston labor history, see James V. Reese, "The Early History of Labor Organizations in Texas, 1838–1876," *Southwest Historical Quarterly* 72 (July 1968), 1, 8–9; and Allen Clayton Taylor, "A History of the Screwmen's Benevolent Association from 1866–1924" (M.A. thesis, University of Texas, Austin, 1968).

CHAPTER ONE

In addition to the general references on the storm cited above, all of which devote significant space to accounts of the hurricane, numerous manuscript sources from the Galveston and Texas History Center of Rosenberg Library provide first-person accounts of the event itself. A notebook index of manuscript sources on the storm facilitates navigation of the collection. The holdings of the Galveston County Historical Museum also contain letters and reminiscences from the storm and recovery. Additional narratives were found in other repositories. The Gid Scherer letter may be found in the Charles W. Hutson Papers, no. 362, at the Southern Historical Collection, Wilson Library, the University of North Carolina at Chapel Hill, and several accounts came from the Center for

American History at the University of Texas at Austin. Copies of Isaac Cline's report on the storm may be found at Rosenberg Library, and his autobiography, *Storms, Floods, and Sunshine* (New Orleans: Pelican Press, 1945), contains a chapter on his service in Galveston. Immediately after the storm, numerous grisly, horrific, and somewhat fictional tabloid accounts of the disaster appeared on the market. These were largely responsible for the popular image of the hurricane and its survivors; see for example, Paul Lester, *The Great Galveston Disaster* (Philadelphia: Globe, 1900); John Coulter, ed., *The Complete Story of the Galveston Horror, Written by the Survivors* (Chicago: United Publishers of America, 1900); Nathan C. Greene, ed., *Story of the Galveston Flood: Complete, Graphic, Authentic* (Baltimore: R. H. Woodward Co., 1900); and Murat Halstead, *Galveston: The Horrors of a Stricken City* (Chicago: American Publishers Association, 1900). Clarence Ousley compiled and edited *Galveston in 1900* (Atlanta: W. C. Chase, 1901) as a corrective to these sensationalist accounts and to raise money for the public schools.

CHAPTER TWO

To obtain the best overall understanding of the post-storm recovery, readers should begin with David G. McComb, *Galveston: A History* (Austin: University of Texas Press, 1986); John Edward Weems, *A Weekend in September* (College Station: Texas A&M University Press, 1957, 1980); Harold M. Hyman, *Oleander Odyssey: The Kempners of Galveston, Texas, 1854–1980s* (College Station: Texas A&M University Press, 1990); Clarence Ousley, *Galveston in 1900* (Atlanta: W. C. Chase, 1900); and Stephen P. Kretzmann, "A House Built Upon the Sand: Race, Class, Gender, and the Galveston Hurricane of 1900" (Ph.D. dissertation, University of Wisconsin, Madison, 1995). There is no better way to interpret the urgency and realism of the disaster than to read the issues of the Galveston *Daily News* and the Galveston *Tribune* surrounding the hurricane. The *Report of the Central Relief Committee for Galveston Storm Sufferers* (Galveston, 1902) is valuable for reconstructing the city's relief efforts, as is the *Report of Red Cross Relief, Galveston, Texas* (Washington, D.C., 1900–1901), written by Clara Barton and various members of the Galveston Red Cross relief team and available at the Galveston and Texas History Center of the Rosenberg Library. Also helpful was Ellen Beasley, *The Alleys and Back Buildings of Galveston: An Architectural and Social History* (Houston: Rice University Press, 1996). The Galveston and Texas History Center of the Rosenberg Library is the best site to begin seeking primary documents related to the city's disaster. Well organized and easily accessible for the researcher, the history center is the repository for manuscript collections that detail the events of the storm and recovery through official governmental reports, individual impressions, business accounts, family papers, and photographs. Of particular help was the carefully compiled list of manuscript collections that related to the storm and its aftermath, including the following: the Louisa Rollfing Biography, the Ben Stuart Papers, and the J. H. Hawley Papers. The Center for American History, University of Texas at Austin, also holds useful photograph and manuscript collections, such as the Henry Wolfram Papers, the Galveston Screwmen's Benevolent Association Records, and the Henry Cohen Papers.

Our discussion of Clara Barton and the Red Cross began with biographies: Elizabeth Brown Pryor, *Clara Barton: Professional Angel* (Philadelphia: University of Pennsylvania Press, 1987); and Ishbel Ross, *Angel of the Battlefield: The Life of Clara Barton* (New York: Harper, 1956). Red Cross policies were explained in J. Byron Deacon, *Disasters and the American Red Cross in Disaster Relief* (New York: Russell Sage Foundation, 1918). The most valuable records for detailing the Red Cross role in Galveston are the Clara Barton Papers, on microfilm from the Manuscript Division of the Library of Congress. Discussion of the New York fund raisers for the Galveston public schools and for the Galveston orphans came from *The New York Times* and Mrs. Roger A. Pryor, *My Day: Reminiscences of a Long Life* (New York: Macmillan, 1909).

Helpful sources for reconstructing African American history and the recovery are George P. Rawick, ed., *The American Slave: A Composite Autobiography* (Westport, Conn.: Greenwood, 1979); and the Galveston *City Times*. For women's history and the creation of the WHPA, begin with Elizabeth Hayes Turner, *Women, Culture, and Community: Religion and Reform in Galveston, 1880–1920* (New York: Oxford University Press, 1997); the Morgan Family Papers, Rosenberg Library; and the Margaret Sealy Burton Letters, Center for American History, University of Texas at Austin.

CHAPTER THREE

Any account of Galveston's shift to the commission form of government must begin with Bradley R. Rice, "The Galveston Plan of City Government by Commission: The Birth of a Progressive Idea," *Southwestern Historical Quarterly* 78 (April 1975), 365–408. Rice expands his account in his *Progressive Cities: The Commission Government Movement in America, 1901–1920* (Austin: University of Texas Press, 1977). Other views of the

decision may be found in David G. McComb, *Galveston: A History* (Austin: University of Texas Press, 1986); Harold M. Hyman, *Oleander Odyssey: The Kempners of Galveston, Texas, 1854–1980s* (College Station: Texas A&M University Press, 1990); and Stephen P. Kretzmann, "A House Built Upon the Sand: Race, Class, Gender, and the Galveston Hurricane of 1900" (Ph.D. dissertation, University of Wisconsin, Madison, 1995). Copies of the Robert, Ripley, and Noble engineering report may be found in several different collections at Rosenberg Library as well as other manuscript sources containing images and texts describing construction and expansion of the sea wall. The Edmund R. Cheesborough Papers, the Galveston County Board of Engineers Records, the Campbell Family Papers, and the Trueheart Papers, also at Rosenberg Library, are the best sources of information on the grade raising. In addition to scrapbooks with newspaper clippings and some official documentation, letterpress volumes in the Cheesborough collection record the bulk of his correspondence as secretary of the grade raising board. The logbook of the dredge *Texas*, which sank on the way to Galveston, is also located at the Rosenberg Library. The Galveston County Historical Museum possesses both photographic and manuscript materials about the sea wall and grade raising, including architectural drawings. The regional branch of the National Archives in Fort Worth, Texas, has a scrapbook of photographs from 1905 that captures both damage caused by the 1900 Storm and the process of constructing the sea wall in front of Fort Crockett. One of the most fruitful sources of information was a cache of documents purchased at a local antique store which included a copy of a paper on the history of the sea wall produced by the Corps of Engineers for delivery at a conference and later public release, as well as Florence Vedder's self-published memoir. *Engineering News* and the *Engineering Record*, trade journals for the profession, kept up with both the sea wall and grade raising, and periodic articles outlined both process and progress with useful maps and drawings. For the role of engineers in the project an article by Stanley K. Schultz and Clay McShane, "To Engineer the Metropolis: Sewers, Sanitation, and City Planning in Late-Nineteenth-Century America," *Journal of American History* 65 (September 1978), 389–411, explains the clout of professional engineers in the new field of urban planning. As environmental studies grows as a field of investigation, a number of works outlining the role of the U.S. Army Corps of Engineers in coastal development have appeared, including Orrin H. Pilkey and Katherine L. Dixon, *The Corps and the Shore* (Durham, N.C.: Duke University Press, 1996), and most recently, Cornelia

Dean, *Against the Tide* (New York: Columbia University Press, 1999). John Barry's *Rising Tide* (New York: Simon and Schuster, 1997) focuses on the devastating 1927 flood of the Mississippi, but also contains useful information on the evolution of the Corps and its interaction with private sector projects. Lynn M. Alperin, *Custodians of the Coast: History of the United States Army Engineers at Galveston* (Galveston: U.S. Corps of Engineers, 1977), is an invaluable account of the Galveston District.

CHAPTER FOUR

For reconstructing Galveston's economic and political recovery we relied upon the Galveston city newspapers and Galveston city directories published annually by Morrison and Fourmy Directory Company; Harold M. Hyman, *Oleander Odyssey: The Kempners of Galveston, Texas* (College Station: Texas A&M University Press, 1990); David G. McComb, *Galveston: A History* (Austin: University of Texas Press, 1986); and trade, port, and manufacturing publications from the years 1902 until 1916.

The literature on the city commission plan of government that was most helpful to this chapter included Bradley R. Rice, *Progressive Cities: The Commission Government Movement in America, 1901–1920* (Austin: University of Texas Press, 1977); Rice, "The Galveston Plan of City Government by Commission: The Birth of a Progressive Idea," *Southwestern Historical Quarterly* 78 (April 1975), 365–408; James Weinstein, "Organized Business and the City Commission and Manager Movements," *Journal of Southern History* 27 (May 1962), 166–182; Samuel P. Hays, "The Politics of Reform in Municipal Government in the Progressive Era," *Pacific Northwest Quarterly* 55 (1965), 157–169; Hays, "The Changing Political Structure of the City in Industrial America," *Journal of Urban History* 1 (1974), 6–38; and Clinton Rogers Woodruff, ed., *City Government by Commission* (New York, 1914). For Jewish immigrants to the Midwest see Bernard Marinbach, *Galveston: Ellis Island of the West* (Albany: State University of New York Press, 1983); and the Henry Cohen Papers, Center for American History, University of Texas at Austin. The history of Galveston's Mardi Gras may be found in the vertical files of the History Center of the Rosenberg Library and in the Margaret Sealy Burton Letters, Center for American History, University of Texas at Austin.

For a more detailed survey of the Women's Health Protective Association see Elizabeth Hayes Turner, *Women, Culture, and Community: Reli-gion and Reform in Galveston, 1880–1920* (New York: Oxford University Press, 1997); as well as *Constitution and By-laws of the Women's Health Protective Association of Galveston* (Galveston: Clarke and Courts, 1901); the Morgan Family Papers; and *Report of a Sanitary Survey of the City of Galveston, Texas* (Galveston: 1913), in the Rosenberg Library. To learn more about pure food and milk nationally and in Texas see Mitchell Okun, *Fair Play in the Marketplace: The First Battle for Pure Food and Drugs* (Dekalb, Ill.: Northern Illinois University Press, 1986); and Megan Seaholm, "Earnest Women: The White Woman's Club Movement in Progressive Era Texas, 1880–1920" (Ph.D. dissertation, Rice University, 1988).

The literature on the woman suffrage movement in Texas is growing. Two helpful publications are Ruthe Winegarten and Judith N. McArthur, eds., *Citizens at Last: The Woman Suffrage Movement in Texas* (Austin: Ellen C. Temple, 1987); and Judith N. McArthur, *Creating the New Woman: The Rise of Southern Women's Progressive Culture in Texas, 1893–1918* (Urbana and Chicago: University of Illinois Press, 1998). See also Patricia B. Nieuwenhuizen, "Minnie Fisher Cunningham and Jane Y. McCallum: Leaders of Texas Women for Suffrage and Beyond" (Senior thesis, University of Texas at Austin, 1982); and Anastatia Sims, "The Woman Suffrage Movement in Texas" (Senior thesis, University of Texas at Austin, 1974). Information on the Galveston's woman suffrage movement may be found in Turner, *Women, Culture, and Community*; and Larry J. Wygant, "'A Municipal Broom': The Woman Suffrage Campaign in Galveston, Texas," *Houston Review* 6 (No. 3, 1984), 117–134.

For the history of African Americans in Texas see Alwyn Barr, *Black Texans: A History of Negroes in Texas, 1528–1971* (Austin: University of Texas Press, 1973); Lawrence D. Rice, *The Negro in Texas, 1874–1900* (Baton Rouge: Louisiana State University Press, 1971). For Galveston African Americans see Galveston *City Times*; Galveston *New Idea*; Galveston *Daily News*; Betty Massey, ed., *Black Galvestonians: A Glimpse of the Past, a Challenge for the Future* (Galveston, n.d); Leon A. Morgan, *Public Education for Blacks in Galveston, 1838–1968* (Galveston, 1978); "Handbook, Colored Branch," 1918, and Minutes, Rosenberg Library Association, both in Rosenberg Library Papers; and the Bert Armstead Papers, Rosenberg Library. Minutes for the Hospital Aid Society are in the possession of Mrs. Izola Collins, Galveston.

INDEX